Careers in Computing and Information Technology

Careers in Computing and Information Technology

Eric Deeson

Kogan Page

First published in Great Britain
in 1987 by Kogan Page Limited,
120 Pentonville Road, London N1 9JN

British Library Cataloguing in Publication Data
Deeson, Eric
Careers in computing and information technology.
I. Computer industry – Vocational Guidance – Great Britain 2. Computer service industry – Vocational guidance – Great Britain
I. Title
004' .023'41 QA76.25

ISBN 1-85091-265-3

Typeset by V&M Graphics Ltd, Aylesbury, Bucks
Printed and bound in Great Britain by
The Camelot Press Ltd, Southampton

Contents

Part 2

Acknowledgements

For their help in the preparation of this book I have many people to thank: Jacquetta Megarry, Eileen Young and my wife Cynthia have provided much useful advice. Doreen Goodwin of Warwick Systems of Birmingham saved my life with masses of information, while Lynne Nicholls, my indefatigable word processor, put in many hours preparing the text of the book.

Those who provided particular help in the form of hard information and comment also deserve gratitude. They are Evelyn Dickey of The Boots Company; Dr N Kitchen, Unilever's recruitment manager; W H Scriven, personnel manager of the Filton division of British Aerospace; J G Simpson of ICI's Group personnel department; S Smith of the Ministry of Defence; the personnel department of Ford Motor Company.

This book is a completely revised version of Kogan Page's *Careers in Computers and New Information Technology* by Dennis Carlyle. Complete revision or not, I must say that that book was so good that I was able to lift whole sections with little change, so I must express my thanks to Dennis Carlyle too for all his immense effort a few years ago.

I am indebted to the magazine *Computer Weekly* for kind permission to use data for the figures on pages 56, 118, 119 and 120.

Finally, I turn to the most important person of all: you. I wish you every success with your career and hope that this book provides a lot of useful information and help. But do me a favour, please: if I've left things out, or made actual errors, that you think other people should know about, let me know. Then the next edition of this little book can be even more helpful and useful. Write to me via the publisher, Kogan Page Ltd (120 Pentonville

Road, London N1 9JN), and then look out for your name in print when I add you to my list of people to thank!

Eric Deeson
Birmingham
January 1987

Foreword

Industries related to information technology (IT), including particularly the computer industry, are among the world's fastest growing. They will remain so for some decades to come. Computers (the main area of IT covered in this book) are developing at an amazing rate which shows no signs of slowing. Their use is spreading fast into and through every other industry, and every field of human activity: businesses of all sizes (from the biggest banks, offices and factories to the corner shop and the one-person plumbing firm); research and development in every area of science and technology; all aspects of international co-operation, national government and local government (yes, even down to parish level); education, health care, services and utilities; the home. Because of this enormous and rapid expansion there just aren't enough people to work in IT and with computers; this is true of nearly every area and it will remain true for a good while yet.

Few people appreciate the extent to which the information revolution has changed society already. Even fewer appreciate how much further that revolution has still to go (some aspects of these matters are explored in Chapter 1). At the heart of the information revolution is the computer and the fast-growing network of world and local telecommunications; at the heart of that lies the silicon chip, that miraculous (and miraculously cheap) symbol of microelectronics technology. Chapter 2 is the place for the technical background you may like to think about before looking for work in the IT world.

Argument about the outcome of this revolution will range back and forth for longer than our lifetimes. On the one hand, people fear massive unemployment and the dangers of central control of society and the individual. On the other, people look forward to our release from the tyranny of a daily grind and to a major increase in world wealth and standards of living. Whatever the future brings, there's no doubt that it will be based firmly on IT; there's no doubt that people who accept and welcome computers and telecommunications, whatever their work and way of life, will be in great demand. Where that demand lies, with particular reference to work with computers, is the theme of Chapters 3–6. At the end of each is an indication of early 1987 salary levels. The values shown there can give only a rough guide: not only is there great variation between organisations and between parts of the country, but in this business salaries change faster than in most. You will not need to look long at relevant adverts to get the point.

Two warnings before we get on with the book. First, don't think that work with computers is open only to people with high qualifications like degrees in computer science: there are jobs for all who have enough interest and are prepared to put a lot of effort into finding out more about this exciting field. Second, don't think that work in IT is just for males. Far from it: women can, and do, do well in every area explored in this book. Females have as much chance to get in and to get on. All that is said in Chapters 7–10 about getting work and making progress applies just as much to women as to men. The major drawback to a fully integrated workforce is that women hesitate to apply for posts in areas that seem to be male dominated; indeed, it is still true that women do not seek further or higher education in large numbers in many subjects that are relevant here. That means that if you are a female trying to enter some of the careers mentioned in this book, you will have a greater chance of success.

Part 1

Chapter 1

Information Technology and Your Career

Information Revolution

In the last two or three decades the world has seen a revolution in the handling of information: collection, storage, transfer from one place to another, processing, usage and presentation. Indeed, most people think that the information revolution (which is still going on and will make much more progress by the time you retire) is as important in human history as the so-called industrial revolution.

The industrial revolution involved a change from the use of muscle power to the use of machines. The information revolution will reduce greatly the use of paper in favour of electronic systems. The big difference between the two transitions in human history is that the industrial revolution lasted centuries, but the one we are in now is only a few decades long. Already, it is rare for people to follow the same careers as their parents (that was normal before the end of the industrial revolution). The speed of the information revolution means that soon most people will not be able to expect to keep the same jobs all their lives. Retraining will be needed more and more often, and many people will change jobs, or even careers, two or three times in their working lives.

What has been said applies in all walks of life. However you spend your adult years, as home-maker or hairdresser, farmer or physiotherapist, trader or teacher, you will need to take more account of information technology (IT). That is because every aspect of human life depends on information: no area is free of the need to handle information. (Perhaps the only exception is the hermit who takes nothing with him to his cell, but even he will depend on the information he learned in the past to survive in the future.)

Every time you open a book or look at a paper, every time you use the phone, television or radio, every time you write or get a letter, every time you check a timetable or get a ticket, every time you receive money from pay packet or bank and every time you spend anything you are involved in information technology. There may not seem to be much of a revolution in those examples: your parents did much the same thing in much the same way. Yet modern IT is changing them fast already.

Much of the information stored in books, papers and timetables is now also stored electronically. It is becoming easier to use IT to obtain such information quickly and cheaply, and the information is more up-to-date.

Telephone and broadcasting systems are becoming more versatile, more efficient and able to do more things. Perhaps you have joined in a radio phone-in programme, used teletext to find out things on a special television set or heard of someone who uses the phone to talk to people on the other side of the world as easily as those on the other side of the street. All these show modern IT at work. IT is also beginning to replace letters by electronic mail, personal telex messages and facsimile transmissions (fax) that can send copies of documents and drawings across the oceans in seconds.

Credit cards, electronic tills in the walls of the banks, automatic transfer of the cost of your purchases from your bank to the shop: these uses of IT in the handling of money reduce wasted time and trouble. They reduce too the need to handle cash and thus improve security. IT is changing every aspect of our lives. Personally, we may hardly notice, and can often even choose not to join in, but in employment you will notice and almost certainly you will have to join in.

What is Information Technology?

As mentioned already modern IT concerns all aspects of the handling of information: collection, storage, transfer, processing, usage and presentation. While pen and paper, smoke signals and counting marks on the bark of trees are truly IT, our prime interest is in electronic information-handling.

There are three strands to that technology: microelectronics, telecommunications and computing. (The use of technical words will be kept to a minimum, but note that at the end of Chapter 2 there is a little glossary of IT words and phrases. If you decide to look for a career in these areas, you'll need to become familiar with them.) These three strands are linked together closely in the strong IT thread. It is the aim of people developing IT systems to bring them even closer together, to make one integrated easy-to-use system. When they succeed, and when that system is cheap, universal and very easy to use, the information revolution will be over. It won't take long. However, while they are still a bit separate, let us look at these three strands of IT. Don't forget the end of Chapter 2 if there are words you don't know!

MICROELECTRONICS

Microelectronics concerns the design, building and use of circuits and systems that use tiny electric currents. An ordinary electric circuit, like that of a house light bulb, runs on between a quarter and half an ampere of current. Microelectronics circuits use a thousandth of that, or even far less.

Years ago, radio sets used more electricity than modern TV sets; a portable radio was almost too heavy to lift and could run for only a few hours on a car battery. Now we have all kinds of equipment based on microelectronics: audio and video systems, clocks and watches, cameras and calculators, controllers in all kinds of domestic equipment and computers. All these types of equipment are becoming cheaper, smaller, more powerful and more reliable year by year, all because of progress in microelectronics. All use less and less energy. Each year too brings more equipment no one dreamed of a decade ago (the pocket TV set, the personal cassette-player, the computer on a wristband, the throw-away camera, the car that tells you to fasten your seatbelt), all because of microelectronics.

Modern microelectronic systems are built around the little black beetle-like chips (integrated circuits) that you may have seen inside a TV set or computer. Costing only a few pence to make, chips are amazingly complex three-dimensional circuits. If you were to magnify one of those circuits so it looked like the street map of a town, it would cover the whole country. As it is, the integrated circuit itself is little more than the size of a matchhead.

TELECOMMUNICATIONS

Telecommunications concerns the transfer of information from place to place without people having to carry it. Telephones, radio and TV come in here; all are being revolutionised by microelectronic 'magic'. The old, slow, heavy and unreliable cables are giving way to new, fast, light reliable ones a tenth or a hundredth the size. Satellites are coming more and more to share the load, and no satellite could reach orbit without computers.

COMPUTING

Apart from the domestic equipment listed above, computers are the most well-known result of the information revolution. All modern ones are microelectronic systems, and they appear in every part of all telecommunications equipment. In this book we shall concentrate mainly on work with computers rather than with microelectronics or telecommunications as such.

Careers and IT

It is clear that IT is coming to affect everybody's work, whatever their work may be. Truly therefore a book called *Careers in Computing and Information Technology* should tell you about every career there is. That would hardly help you, so this book is restricted on the whole to careers that involve computers directly. We shall touch on aspects of the microelectronics and telecommunications industries. Also, of course, we shall try to keep the thread of IT, for no other reason than that by the end of your working life, if not well before then, the three strands of IT will be woven together very tightly.

The computing industry has two main parts. The first one is production and includes research, design, development, manufacture, sales, servicing and repair. It is particularly close to microelectronics within the overall IT field and is looked at in Chapter 6, but if that is where your interest lies, I hope you'll still read through the other chapters before it. Most of these chapters concern the second part of the computing industry, applications, areas in which computers are used all the time and have a central crucial role. This time we are closer to telecommunications than to microelectronics though, of course, some aspects of design, maintenance and servicing require knowledge of the latter field.

It is possible that you picked up this book because already you are excited about IT and/or using computers. IT *is* exciting, in itself and because it is the centre of a major revolution all over the world. Success in an IT career certainly can make you rich and even famous. Even if you don't turn out to have the flair, ideas and success of Sir Clive Sinclair you can find yourself in a very well paid and enjoyable job.

However, it is important to make it clear that the computer is not a magic carpet that can move you to a glittering world. Most jobs to do with IT and computers are no better paid than others that require the same level of qualifications and experience. In some areas indeed there is unemployment; in only a few is there a truly desperate shortage of suitable people. (There is no point in giving a list of either of these; no book, even one updated as often as this, can be accurate in this regard in this rapidly changing industry.)

One thing therefore that must be made clear at this stage is that the computing industry is not a magic city whose streets are paved with gold. Of course, a few people have done extremely well without qualifications and without any more resources than a good imagination and a home computer, but such people are few and they are becoming fewer. To get on in an IT-related career, as in any other, you require qualifications, hard work and personal skills.

A second thing to make clear is that computer people are not all males. In many areas there are actually more females and in most careers considered in this book females can progress just as well as males. There is no evidence that women are less able to understand and use computers than men (though as in every field of technology and business there is still quite a lot of prejudice, on both sides). There are many women who have achieved success in computer-related careers and your having a young family need be no drawback. Indeed, if females do have some different abilities, skills and interests from males, they can be a positive advantage. So, whether you are female or male, do understand that all in this book applies to you! The important thing to realise is that to get on you must enjoy your work and develop your knowledge and skills with interest.

The Future

Most people view a career as involving work within one area for life. You have been warned already that you must be prepared for retraining and even for one or more major changes of job. However, that warning was made for everyone in work. IT may be the cause of those needs, but IT-based industries can in fact be more stable than the rest. The reason for this is that as the industrial revolution moved very large numbers of people from farming to manufacture, so the information revolution is moving large numbers of people into the rapidly growing industries concerned with information. Companies working with IT are growing and they are becoming more numerous. The biggest problem is of a particular company coming to hard times because it doesn't change fast enough. Change is an everyday part of IT industries. Because of this fact, retraining is more common and more efficient in them than elsewhere. Also, because the change involves growth, personal advancement can be more rapid and less painful.

At the end of the last section it was stated that 'The important thing to realise is that to get on you must enjoy your work and develop your knowledge and skills with interest'. Developing your knowledge and skills includes the need to be prepared for change and to accept it. Indeed, most important of all abilities may be to look forward to possible changes and to be able to judge their importance. The more you can plan your career path in advance, the further you will tread.

Insecurity is a problem, then. However, it is far less a problem in the areas discussed in this book than in areas where industry is declining for one reason or another. Try to predict, as you grow older, the areas of decline as well as those where new opportunities are likely. All we can predict is that those three strands of IT mentioned already will come closer together and that the information industries will grow. Life for everyone will become easier and more prosperous, even for those without jobs; working days, weeks, years and lives will become shorter and the home will grow in importance as an integral part of society. Other trends will be picked out in the next few chapters.

Qualifications

It is believed widely that only highly qualified people can obtain jobs with computers and IT. Not true! There are many openings for people with only a few good CSEs, O level/standard grades or GCSE results. Office work, sales and maintenance/servicing (including technicians' work) offer plenty of such openings in particular. The Youth Training Scheme (YTS) is a good way in here, and we return to the point in Chapter 7. Of course, as with all careers, the higher your qualifications, the higher you can enter and the faster you can progress. An A level pass or two will give extra advantage or give you the chance to go to college, polytechnic or university and obtain even higher qualifications.

At whatever stage you stop full-time learning, don't close your eyes to the possibility of following other courses later on. Certainly, if the people you work with offer training, further training, or retraining programmes, think about them with care, even if they need study in your spare time. After all, not only should such work help you progress in your company (for people will respect you for it), it will also be valuable if you decide to look for work somewhere else.

The same applies to courses that may be available in your community, at evening classes or in local schools, libraries, open learning centres, colleges or universities. At the end of the book details are given of where you can find out about such opportunities. Note that your trade union or professional association probably offers useful courses too. In this section we should also mention the new Open College and the Open University. Courses offered by them require a great deal of hard work in your spare time, but the qualifications you can end up with can be extremely valuable.

Another myth to explode is that you must know a lot about computing to enter a computer-related career. That's not true either! Even if you decide to study computing at university, you don't need to have followed any course in the subject before, at school or college. Indeed, you do not need to be a university computer-science graduate to enter the computing industry at high level.

Most important is to have English with a good grade in GCSE or equivalent. The same qualification in mathematics is also needed if you want to study physics, technology or computing at A level or at university. Useful subjects at any level are business studies, commerce, accounting, office practice and physics. At A level, polytechnic or university think too about economics, statistics, electrical or mechanical engineering and electronics. Courses anywhere in any of these will provide plenty of opportunity for you to use and explore computers.

However, many people think that the most important qualification of all for entry into modern IT work is to be able to use a keyboard effectively. Certainly, if you can type well, you have a major advantage as far as entry to data preparation and the electronic office are concerned; adequate typing ability is of value in every job at every level now that keyboards are so common. On the other hand, do not be despondent if you are a slow keyboard pecker rather than a hundred-word-a-minute speeder: it may well be that within ten years the keyboard will have been replaced by other better ways of communicating with equipment.

Chapter 2

Background IT

What is a Computer?

Ok, we can hear you muttering the question, 'what's the point of background theory?' After all, if you get a book on stamp collecting, the author doesn't try to take up your time with lots of details of printing processes through the ages. Please don't reject the material in the rest of this chapter, however – it's important. Computing is not like stamp collecting: here you are trying to control a set of complex electronic equipment and it helps to know a little bit about it.

Anyway, it is possible (whether you've ever studied information technology at school or college or not) that interviewers may try to find out something of your basic knowledge as well as interest in the field. Most of this chapter, like most of the book, is concerned with computers, but is followed up by a couple of sections on the other aspects of IT: microelectronics and telecommunications.

The chapter closes with a glossary of short notes on the various technical terms met here or elsewhere. There is no need to learn all this material, but basic knowledge will help you with interviews, settling in at your work and your future career.

So what is a computer? The first thing you need to know is that there are lots of kinds of computer. Probably, you have some around your home already, inside things like digital watches, electronic calculators and video games or giving sophisticated features in a modern cooker, sewing machine or video tape-recorder. All these, however, contain special-purpose computers, complex electronic chips dedicated to a special task in each case. A computer of the type with which we are concerned, on the other hand, is general purpose: given suitable instructions and attachments, it can do the work of any dedicated machine. If you've been able to try a home or school microcomputer with a few programs, you may have found it used for timing, calculating, gaming and so on; suitable instructions within the programs of a general-purpose computer can handle all kinds of things.

In summary, then, a general-purpose computer can do many different things when instructed properly. A special-purpose computer is dedicated to a small range of functions and cannot (easily) have its instructions changed.

A modern computer is a general-purpose, high speed, digital electronic, stored-program data processor.

General purpose has been explained already, but what about all those other terms?

HIGH SPEED

Allied with its accuracy, the high speed of operation of a computer is a crucial feature. Indeed, people have been looking for centuries for machines to offer such facilities to help them in their work. Computers can in fact do things much faster than people and they don't get tired, go on strike or have off-days either. Modern microcomputers can carry out thousands, or even many millions, of actions each second. That means that they can do very complex operations very quickly and also keep up with fast-changing situations.

STORED PROGRAM

A program is an ordered set of instructions for a computer to carry out. (Note that the spelling is not programme, by the way; the American spelling is used here to distinguish the computing word from the broadcast one.) Just think what it would be like to give the machine each instruction in turn, when it is able to carry out millions in a second: the microcomputer would be sitting around for almost 100 per cent of the time waiting for the human operator to tell it the next thing to do. That would be a great waste of its potential and not many people would feel like using computers if that had to be done. So the computer must be able to store the program instructions somehow, so that it can carry them out in a flash on demand. It needs a place to hold them, and that place we call the store. The fact that computers can recall instructions for use on demand is what makes them so important.

DIGITAL ELECTRONIC

All digital electronic means is that this is an electronic system like your TV set or bedside clock/radio, working on tiny electric currents. (Actually, the computer's currents are really tiny, and therefore is a microelectronic device.) The digital bit refers to the fact that the currents run around in pulses rather than in a continuous stream. Pulses can be counted, which means they can act like numbers. The word digits means numbers and the word computer means something for calculating.

DATA PROCESSOR

Data processing is what computing's all about. Any computer processes data (which represent information that people are interested in) to produce more data (more interesting information).

Most computers can be used by only one person at a time, with only one keyboard and screen. Home computers are like this, as are the ones used generally in schools and colleges. We call such a one-person machine a micro (or microcomputer). Micros are very cheap and reliable; however, they often have a fairly small memory and don't work very fast. All the same, today's cheapest micros are far in advance, in these and other ways, of the world's biggest machines a few decades ago.

One way to overcome some of the problems that follow the micro's being usable by only one person at a time is to link a number into a group called a network. (More and more schools and colleges are getting networks, and they are becoming common in office systems too.) The users of a network can share costly little-used resources like a large storage unit or a high quality printer; often they will also be able to communicate with each other to some extent through their individual computers.

The number of networks is growing fast though their use is fairly new.

There is a second way to provide multi-user capability, and that involves the use of the minicomputer. This is a central unit with a large storage system able to support up to a dozen individual users at once. Each user (who may be some distance from the centre, linked by a special cable) has a keyboard and display and will feel as if he or she is using the system alone. Such a combination of keyboard and display often goes by the name of terminal or VDU (visual display unit), the latter especially if the two are in a single box. A VDU may have some storage and processing power of its own (then it's called an intelligent VDU) and may run a printer. The place where this equipment is sited is called the user's work station.

The most powerful computers, called mainframes, can support hundreds or even thousands of users. The biggest difference between mainframes and smaller systems is that they need fairly full-time staffing to keep all their many facilities working fully.

Hardware and Software

All digital computers have the same basic structure. It's true of your Spectrum, it's true of the massive multi-million pound machines used by the Pentagon and the Inland Revenue for their seedy purposes and it's true of the huge but feeble machines of the 1940s.

The section of the overall computer system that does the actual hard work is called the processor or, in full, the central processing unit (CPU). Its job is to process electronic data in the form of electrical numbers; the part of the processor that deals with this is the arithmetic and logic unit (ALU); next to it in the central processor is the control unit that conducts the whole operation.

What does the central processor process?: data. How does it know what to do?: through programs. Data and programs must be stored, so close to the processor is the main store or memory. If you've tried typing in a program to a micro, you'll have realised that keyboard entry is not the best way to give computers instructions. Bear in mind, after all, that there are millions of

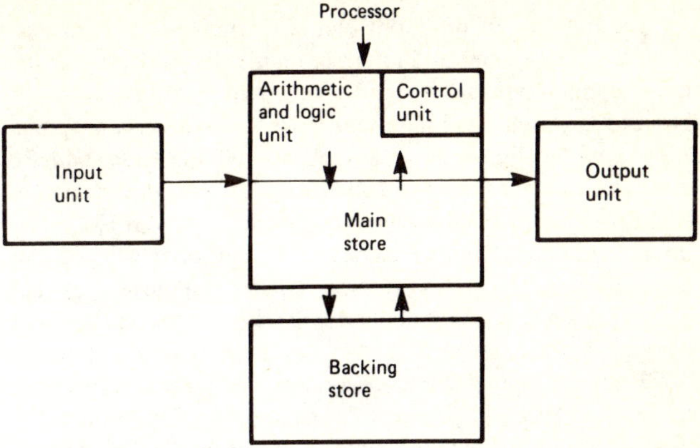

different tasks that a general-purpose computer could be expected to do, so there are millions of possible programs. All but the very simplest computers therefore have an extra memory, the so-called backing store. In the case of home and school machines this can be a cassette recorder and cassettes, a disc system or cartridges – and it's just the same with the systems used in other areas of life.

All computers must also be in communication with their users. Each user wants to be able to feed in commands, programs and data. The input unit deals with that need; in most cases this unit is, of course, a keyboard. Also, the computer has to be able to give the user messages and data: it needs an output unit. The TV screen or monitor that we are able to use at home is a standard output unit for microcomputers. (A printer is another one.) The way that all these bits fit together is shown in the figure above. It's noteworthy that people often call the input/output units and backing store the computer's peripherals (outside parts).

Peripherals

The central processing unit of a computer (arithmetic unit, control unit, main store and so on) can't be of any use to people without the peripherals. These comprise input and output units (maybe joined into a VDU) plus the backing store. Each of those three parts can take various forms.

The function of the input unit is to allow the user to feed commands, programs and information into the CPU. By far the most common type is some kind of keyboard or keypad, but voice input is growing in importance, especially in certain special situations. The light-pens used with bar codes in shops and the machines that read the magnetic ink characters on cheques, as well as the touch screen systems you may have seen on TV, are all input techniques. Others include special pads on which you can draw or write information to the computer and the sensors that tell automated systems like robots what they need to know about the outside world.

As far as output systems are concerned (those which carry out the reverse process of passing information from CPU to user) the most common is some kind of video screen. While the standard TV set is common for use with home micros, outside of that some kind of monitor (or with portable equipment a calculator-style flat-screen display) is the norm. Monitors give far better displays than TV sets and really high quality ones cost thousands of pounds.

Printers form the second most common class of output unit. There are many kinds; they differ in flexibility, speed, quality of output and (of course) price. The most costly ones can output a number of pages a second; these are of great value to mail-marketing companies and for making out bills and receipts in organisations sueh as electricity and telephone companies.

Voice output is growing in importance too: not normally for robots (despite science fiction) but for the computers in cars and in a number of industrial situations. High-quality graphics output on paper is needed in many contexts and special units can provide that too.

Lastly, we turn to methods of backing storage, techniques of storing programs and information in a small space for later use. The punched paper tape and cards you may have heard of in this context are almost never used now, and even the magnetic tape that replaced them is fast disappearing except for back-up purposes. Magnetic discs, like the 'floppies' you may have used at school or college but hard, bigger and normally used several to a pack, provide the normal backing storage media. They are fairly cheap and reliable and allow any given item of information to be accessed very quickly. A mainframe system will often have tens or even hundreds of disc drives joined to the CPU.

Software

All the items described so far (the CPU and a system's range of peripherals) go by the name of hardware: equipment in other words. However, no computer can run without software, the name given to the programs that keep it working properly and instruct it to do what the user wishes.

Software comes in three main groups. To keep a system working properly needs operating software; this is normally included when one buys a computer and includes such systems as MS–DOS and Unix. On top of the operating software are the so-called utilities, which include the programs designed to translate the user's programs into a form the operating software can handle. Programming languages like BASIC, COBOL and Fortran come in here, but there are hundreds of others, including word processors.

The third layer of software for a computer system consists of the user's programs themselves. These are the ones designed to carry out the user's particular tasks. Examples are software to help keep accounts and handle stock control and software for working with graphics, for training and teaching or for the handling of information in various useful ways.

More Microelectronics

You may know that an electric circuit consists of a power source, a switch or other control, a fuse and some device to use the power (like a lamp, kettle or motor). Many circuits include elements such as resistors, capacitors, inductors and diodes for various reasons. A conductor, such as a metal wire, joins the parts. Electronic and microelectronic circuits are much the same in principle. The transistor in its many forms is now the most important element. We use this to store information and to control its transfer in the form of electrical signals.

In an integrated microelectronic circuit, a chip, thousands or even hundreds of thousands of elements are packed together in the surface of a tiny scrap of semiconductor material. The design is such that chips are very small, light, cheap and reliable. They can perform amazing tasks yet use only a very small amount of electricity. Each such tiny scrap of semiconductor, processed to give it all these elements, is far too fragile to be used as it is. Instead it is mounted in a little block of plastic with very small wires joining its edges to the metal legs (pins) of the familiar beetle-like chip.

Often hundreds or thousands of chips are mounted inside bigger electronic circuits to make up a system like a computer's central processor or a video unit. It is a normal for the chips to be soldered on to a plastics sheet with the other elements needed, joined together by metal tracks printed on to the sheet (a printed circuit board).

The technology of the design, manufacture and usage of chips and microelectronic systems is fascinating because they are so small yet so complex. There are many jobs for physics, electronics and engineering graduates here, as well as work for technicians, librarians, office and other such support personnel.

More Telecommunications

As we have seen, this industry concerns the transfer of information over a distance. As far as IT is concerned, the original information (spoken words, graphics or text material on paper, or data stored in a computer, for instance) is converted into an electrical signal. This is done by a transducer (such as a microphone) or an interface.

Normally, the next stage uses an amplifier to make that electrical signal stronger. The signal then passes through a metal cable as an electric current, a fine glass fibre as a beam of light or space as a radio transmission. Perhaps further amplification is needed every so often during the transfer; also there will often be switching units in the telecommunications network to direct each package of information along its correct route.

At the receiving end, perhaps after more amplification and switching, the signal passes to another transducer to convert it into useful energy. This transducer may be a speaker to produce sound waves, a computer screen or some kind of printer. A major problem of telecommunications is interference (called noise) that makes the transmitted information harder to follow. Modern digital systems are much improved in this regard.

Some systems transfer information in one way only; a good example is that of TV broadcasts. Others are two way, an example being the telephone network; we call these two-channel systems or circuits. If there is a lot of signal traffic between two points, certain techniques are used to mix the signals together so as to allow many channels in a single cable. Sometimes thousands of channels can be carried by one cable in this way.

The telecommunications industry is a huge one with many thousands of job vacancies each year. As well as management and a wide range of support staff, the industry needs many technicians, engineers and scientists. It is possible therefore to enter telecommunications research, development, sales, production and maintenance with almost any level of qualification. Qualifications related to physics are valuable particularly for careers on the technical side.

Glossary

Entries here must be very brief, so in some cases you may want or need to look elsewhere for futher details; some other useful books are listed in Chapter 11. However, remember that understanding a little is better than forgetting a lot. Also note that technical words in each entry will themselves appear elsewhere.

ADC. See *Analogue to digital converter.*

*Algorithm.*The solution to a problem set out as an ordered sequence of steps, perhaps in words or in pseudo-code, in graphic form as a flow chart or structure diagram, or in detail as a computer program.

Amplifier. A device to increase the strength of an input signal.

Analogue. Describes a signal that varies smoothly rather than being pulsed (digital).

Analogue to digital converter (ADC). A device with an analogue input and a digital output.

ASCII code. The set of numbers (0–64, 0–128 or sometimes 0–255)

which in many IT systems represents various control effects, letters, digits, punctuation marks and symbols.
Assembler. A program that converts assembly language code into machine code.
Assembly language. A programming language that allows direct control of the processor concerned and its storage sites, but still allows the use of labels.
Audio (voice). In the frequency range up to about 20,000 Hz.

Backing storage. The use of discs and tapes (in most cases) to hold the information in a computer's main store for later use.
Back-up. A security copy of the data on a disc or tape.
Bar code. A series of parallel lines which vary in width and spacing to carry digital information, read into a computer by, for instance, passing a light-pen across it.
BASIC. The most common microcomputer programming language.
Batch. A method of computer operation that allows no interaction with the user: a whole program runs from start to finish without input.
Binary. The counting system used in computer systems, with only two digits (bits): 0 and 1.
Bit. A binary digit, 0 or 1.
Bug. An error in a program.
Burster. A machine that separates continuous computer printout into sheets.
Byte. A set of eight bits, the standard unit of data in many small computers.

CAD. See *Computer-aided design*.
Calculator. A microelectronic device designed for arithmetical and mathematical work with very small memory and often no programmability.
CAM. See *Computer-aided manufacture*.
Central processing unit (CPU). The chip(s) used to control the working of a computer system, plus some storage and circuits for such actions as timing.
Channel. A one-way telecommunications path.
Character. A letter of the alphabet, a number, or some other meaningful symbol (including the space character).

Chip. A complete integrated circuit on a tiny piece of a semiconductor such as silicon.
Code. To convert an outline algorithm into a program in a given computer language; also the name for the program that results.
Communications link. A system that carries information between two machines or people.
Computer. A complete general-purpose system consisting of central processing unit, peripherals and operating software.
Computer-aided design (CAD). The use of high-power computing equipment to help with all aspects of design/tasks.
Computer-aided manufacture (CAM). The use of computer systems to automate manufacturing processes; related to robotics.
Conductor. A substance (in most cases metal) able to carry electric current easily, or a lead made from such a substance.
Console. The main control centre of a computer system, a special terminal with keyboard(s) and display(s), at which the chief operator works.
Control. The use of a computer automatically to look after some aspect of the environment (such as the temperatures of a suite of rooms).
CPU. See *Central processing unit*.

DAC. See *Digital to analogue converter*.
Data. Information as it appears in an information-technology system, without any meaning as such.
Database. A collection of information that can be accessed through a computer system by one or more programs.
Decollater. A machine used to separate the top sheet and copies, and maybe carbon paper, of a printout.
Digital. Describes a signal which comes in pulses (perhaps representing the binary 0 and 1) rather than varying smoothly (analogue).
Digital to analogue converter (DAC). A device with a digital input and an analogue output.
Disc. The most common type of backing storage medium, used in a drive, and holding information in magnetic or optical form.
Documentation. Instructions and other support provided on paper.

Electric. Describes a system in which flows electric charge (current).
Electronic. Describes a system in which the charge flows (currents) are very small.
Electronic till. An automated system giving bank customers information about their accounts and able to provide cash on demand.
Electronics. The science and technology of electronic circuits and systems.
Element. A unit in an electric or electronic circuit or system with one single function.

Feedback. A method by which the output of a device is linked to the input to allow a degree of control.
File. A single collection of information in a computer system.
Flow chart. A graphic view of the structure of a system, process or program.

Graphics. In diagram, graph or picture form, as opposed to text, which mainly consists of characters.

Hardware. The items of equipment which link together to make a computer or other information-technology system.
Hertz (Hz). The unit of frequency for a wave or other alternating signal or sequence of actions, one hertz being a cycle per second.
Hz. See *Hertz.*

Information technology (IT). Concerns the processes and techniques involved in the representation, storage, transfer and use of information for the benefit of people.
Input. Information coming into a system or device and the way it comes in.
Integrated circuit (chip). A large number of electronic elements joined in the surface of a tiny piece of semiconductor (in most cases silicon).
Interaction. Being able to enter information into a running program.
Interface. A device that allows and controls the flow of information from one part of a system to another.
IT. See *Information technology.*

Label. The name given to a section of a computer program or to an item of information held in memory.
LAN. See *Local area network.*
Language. A set of keywords and rules for their use to make a program that will run in a microprocessor or computer system.
Library. The place(s) in a computer installation in which discs or tapes of information and programs are stored.
Local area network (LAN). A network with short (up to 500 m or so) links between the parts.
Low-level language. A programming language not much like a human one but fairly easy for a computer to work with, such as machine code and assembly language.

Machine code. A very low-level programming language, or its results: programs in a form which can be fed directly into and used by a processor, with only numbers to represent instructions and data.
Mainframe. A large computer system able to handle the needs of many users at the same time.
Memory. Where information and programs are stored for use by a computer system.
Microcomputer. A very small computer system able to interact with only one user at a time.
Microelectronics. The science and technology of circuits (especially integrated ones) and of systems working with very small electric currents.
Microprocessor. A central processing unit in a single integrated circuit.
Minicomputer. A small computer system with which several users can work at a time.
Monitor. A high-quality display screen; part of the operating software of a computer system.

Network. A number of computers that are linked, so are able to communicate with each other and to share resources (like printers and databases), close together (local area network) or far apart (wide area network).
Noise. Interference with a signal, making the information it carries less easy to understand.

Operating software. The software usually supplied with a hardware package to control its action.

Package. Hardware and software obtained together for a single main purpose; single-purpose software and its documentation.
PCB. See *Printed circuit board*.
Peripheral. A unit of computer hardware joined (by an interface) to a central processing unit.
Printed circuit board (PCB). A plastics sheet, with conductors printed on to one or both sides, on which can be mounted chips and other circuit elements.
Procedure. A single function part of a program, often one that is used more than once when the program runs; a routine way to carry out a task.
Processing. Changing information (data) from one form to another that is more suitable for a given purpose.
Program. An algorithm (sequence of instructions) coded using a programming language so that a given system can carry it out.
Pseudocode. A form of writing algorithms by using computer programming language concepts and structures but no specific language.

RAM. See *Read and write memory* (sometimes taken to mean random access memory).
Read and write memory (RAM). A system for holding information temporarily: at any time any part can be changed (written to) as well as accessed (read).
Read only memory (ROM). A system for holding information (such as operating software) permanently: it cannot be changed (written to) but only accessed (read).
Record. A single set of information in a file, such as the information about one book in a library's books file.
Robot. A programmable automated machine whose action can include free movement from place to place.
Robotics. The technology of computer control especially as applied to robots.
ROM. See *Read only memory*.

Semiconductor. A material, such as silicon, able to carry current fairly well (but nowhere near as well as a conductor) and with other properties that give it value in microelectronics.

Sensor. A device that detects some form of physical information (such as acidity, light, sound, pressure, strain or magnetism) and gives a corresponding electric output.

Signal. Information in transit, carried by (for instance) electric current, light or radio waves.

Silicon. A semiconductor material, made from sand, used widely as the basis for microelectronic circuits and devices.

Software. Programs and data (information in suitable form) in a computer system.

Storage. Holding programs and data (information in suitable form) for later use, inside the system or (as backing storage) outside.

Suite. A series of separate programs with related purposes and perhaps able to share data; a computer hardware system.

System. A set of separate units (hardware and software) linked to make a working whole.

Telecommunications. The transfer of information over distance by electric or electronic means.

Teletext. A technique for broadcasting information from a database, within, but separate from, television signals; the British systems are Ceefax and Oracle.

Terminal. An input/output system for a single user, linked to a nearby minicomputer or a distant mainframe, that may also have local memory and processing power.

Time sharing. Techniques by which a number of users can work with a single computer system, either when they wish or by taking turns.

Transducer. A sensor of physical information with a corresponding electrical output (examples being photocells and microphone), or the reverse (such as a lamp or a speaker).

VDU. See *Video* (or visual) *display unit*.

Video. Describes the high-frequency signals used in television, for instance, the frequency range being several millions of hertz.

Video display unit (VDU). The most important type of single-user terminal in a large computer system.

Viewdata. A technique for sending information on demand from a central computer database through the telephone network to users' computers, the main British system being Prestel.

Wide area network (WAN). A network spread over large distances.
Window. A section of a computer screen with which the user works while the rest remains fixed but visible and accessible.
Word processing. A computer-based form of typing, in which text entry and editing are simple, and the documents provided by it can be stored for later use.
Work station A terminal or VDU with all the features a single user needs.

Chapter 3

The Electronic Office

What is an Office?

An office is a place where the staff have the role of handling information in many forms. Information comes in, it is processed in to some other form and/or stored, it is used and it goes out. In a very real sense the office is the nerve centre of every organisation; each factory, shop, hospital, government department, farm, bank, restaurant, laboratory (and so on) has one or more offices to handle its information. Indeed, every home has an office, even if it is just a set of papers in the kitchen drawer.

This book opened with the statement that every human activity involves the handling of information: input, process, storage, output. This may be obvious if the activity is running a reference library or a TV news studio, but it is just as true in every other case.

In Chapter 2 it was observed that input, process, storage and output describe the main parts of a computer. Computers are, of course, information processors anyway; that is their job. Because of this, computers have become more widespread in office work than in almost any other area of human activity. The phrase, the electronic office, describes the modern information nerve centre of any organisation, in which people use computers to handle the storage and processing of information and telecommunications to assist with input and output. Probably all offices, except those of most homes and the very smallest business, will be electronic in this sense within a few years.

Word Processing

The word-processor operator is fast replacing the typist; many of the skills are the same, but use of a word processor makes the work easier and more enjoyable. For management, word processing is worthwhile because it allows more work to be done (and to be done better) in a shorter time, and thus provides a more efficient company with a happier staff. The staff in turn has a chance to find out more about the company and its work, so that career development is easier. Thus word-processor operators can become secretaries, office supervisors, librarians, computer operators or management much more easily than traditional typists.

A typist's task is to prepare word-perfect text on paper from handwritten or earlier drafts, from notes, or from dictation (probably on tape). The word-processor operator works with a computer, but has just the same task. There are three main differences, however.

First, it is very simple to change (edit) typed text with a word processor. It is no problem to correct errors, change layout, add or delete material or move chunks of text from one place to another. For a typist, needs like that usually have to be met by starting the document again.

Second, when the document has been typed, it can be printed as a draft for checking, but also it can be stored by the computer in such a way as to make it available for further work at any time in the future. Storage can be in various forms, but even a small floppy disc like some home computers use can store up to 100,000 words of text.

The third advantage of word processing in the electronic office is the link with telecommunications. Instead of having the document printed on paper to be moved physically to its recipient, it can be sent electronically instead. Thus memos can pass around the company, letters can go to suppliers and customers, and reports can reach the people that need them, all within a few seconds and at very low cost. Replies and comments can come back just as quickly from the recipients' computers. IT has certainly revolutionised the office!

To join a firm as a word-processor operator, you should have a few good CSE, O level, standard grade or GCSE passes, including English, as well as typing (40 wpm). Shorthand is dying out, but some people may still welcome it. More important, though, is to have some knowledge of IT and, if possible, some experience of word processing at home, school or college.

CASE STUDIES

Alan is 18 years old and has been with an insurance broker since he left school (with CSE grade 2 English and some experience of typing at home). He started as an office junior but was keen to begin word processing; he was given the chance when one of the office staff left. The company then sent him on a two-day course in the basic principles of word processing with *Wordstar*, that being the system they used then. He didn't find *Wordstar* very easy to work with, but was determined to succeed so kept on improving. He saved up for an Amstrad word-processing system and found that this helped (although it is very different in use). However, that system at home led him to offer his services freelance through a notice in the local supermarket; he now does quite a lot of word processing for students. That isn't very well paid but he finds the experience very valuable and he likes having to type technical material of all kinds.

Meanwhile, at the office Alan's home experience has shown the management that he is hard working and determined to get on. He now does a lot of confidential work as well as the everyday tasks of preparing reports, letters and forms and has a good grasp of the business as well as of the various tasks done in the office.

The managers are thinking of replacing their seven word-processing machines with a network. This will also enable them to use databases and financial software. Alan is very keen to become network manager when this change happens. He has just started a data-processing course at evening classes to prepare himself. (Actually, that might not be the best course for him in the circumstances, but it will certainly be very useful whether he stays or looks for this kind of job in a larger company.)

Doreen's company, a small but growing mail-order supplier of clothing and household goods, introduced a networked computer system in 1985. At the time Doreen (who was then in her mid-twenties) had been with the company a couple of years and, as a general secretary and telephone switchboard operator, had gained a good knowledge of how the company worked.

During the period in which the new computer system was being introduced, all the staff were given courses on its features and use. Doreen became particularly interested in handling records by computer, so she was asked to assist primarily in that aspect of the work. It took a full three months for her and her team to transfer the old paper records on to disc and to ensure that the system was able to handle the company's needs effectively and quickly. A mail-order business needs to be able to use its large collection of customer, stock and supplier records properly and Doreen found that the company introduced several of her ideas for streamlining the system.

Her earliest experience with the switchboard has provided a valuable basis for her involvement with the company's next step. This is to automate communications between the office and the warehouse and the suppliers. The aim is to integrate the stock control and suppliers records so that the computer will automatically telephone orders for more goods when stock levels fall too low. Doreen has recently been given the responsibility of working with the system's designers to bring this about. She has just got Prestel at home (using a simple keyboard as she hasn't a home computer) and has loved finding out about teleshopping. She is sure that teleshopping is a field her company ought to get into, so is now busy in her spare time finding out about how this new kind of mail order could really extend the company's business.

Doreen left school at 16 years old with very few qualifications and spent her first three years working behind the counter of a long series of shops. It was almost an accident that she drifted through catering into becoming an office dogsbody, but now she feels she is really getting somewhere and that she has a bright future. She is right, of course, and it's particularly good that her family are supporting her as she brings more and more work home. It is difficult to know, however, whether she ought to do some suitable evening school work. Perhaps she will find an Open University or Open College course most rewarding and useful for her career?

Data Preparation

Many firms have a huge input of information. Commerce, insurance, finance, travel, utilities (gas, electricity and so on) and council and government departments are typical examples. Organisations like these therefore need offices just to handle that input information efficiently and quickly. They will have large computers to store the data; the job of the data-preparation staff is to convert the input information into a form suitable for the computer.

As the information comes in (by telephone, in letters, as invoices or on other forms) the data-preparation staff type it into the computer system using a keyboard much like that of a word processor. Output on paper is still quite common, but it is fast coming to be normal to have a standard computer screen.

The data-preparation operator's task is rather different from that of the word-processor operator. To be able to type is not so important (but good English and spelling are); it is better to be reliable and fast working. The work can be boring, unless you are dealing direct or by telephone with individual people, but promotion can be rapid even for school-leavers with no qualifications at all.

CASE STUDY

Chris did not leave education at 16 years old but went to a college of further education to do an A level course. At the college she got into bad company and managed to scrape through history only. She was lucky enough (she agrees) to get some part-time work in market research and managed to keep that up while her family grew and grew older. By the time the youngest child started school, Chris had been able to pass a second A level (English). A friend suggested she try to get work with computers and she made personal visits to a number of companies. In fact, it turned out that her own old market-research firm had a vacancy in data preparation, and they were happy to take her on. That was six months ago and she has just got through her probation period so hopes (and expects) to gain a permanent contract.

The market-research company has a large data-preparation department in which Chris is one of over a hundred staff. She finds the work quite a lot less interesting than interviewing, but at least it's warm and comfortable. It is rather boring, though, for her main task each day is to transfer the information from the interview report forms into the computer for analysis. She hopes that she will be able to do well enough to get promotion to some kind of supervisory job. After all, she has read enough to know that market-research forms that computers can read won't be long in coming.

That view is correct, but data-preparation supervision is not necessarily the best she can look forward to. With her background she might actually find a better career in market-research planning and administration. There's plenty of work in that field for people with experience of computers.

Career advancement from data preparation can be into supervisory work, the general office, data control and computer operation. This applies just as much for people who join from school or college with few qualifications or none, though it is particularly important for them to try to gain extra points through training courses or evening classes.

CASE STUDY

Varinder like Chris, and of much the same age, is in data preparation. After leaving school he went from job to job for a while and then became unemployed after a move to another part of the country. He joined an MSC training scheme on which he enjoyed work experience in small offices. At the end of his course eventually he obtained work in data preparation, employed by the local council in a large department.

It took him four years to gain the experience and seniority to allow him to undertake some liaison work with the data-processing staff. He enjoys his visits to the computer block and his meetings with the staff there and now spends much of his time arranging how the work of the two departments can be done most efficiently. This involves learning a lot about the various jobs undertaken by the data-processing department and their various priorities, as well as about how changes in data-collection and -preparation procedures affect data-processing efficiency.

Varinder isn't sure which way he would like to go in the future. Running a data-preparation department certainly has appeal and would let him maintain, if not extend, the links with his computing colleagues. Having a cousin who has done very well in systems analysis inclines him to move more into data processing. That could mean a drop in pay, and he would have to follow some hard training, so he isn't really sure. (It would seem that if Varinder isn't too keen on computing work after he has had so much chance to find out about it, he would be better off if he stayed in data preparation. He could become the manager of a large data preparation department without too much trouble, but would still benefit from suitable further training.)

World of Finance

Banking is much like commerce in many ways. However, while massive levels of information handling are common to both, banks and such organisations also input, process, store and output money. All those tasks to do with money are becoming more and more based on IT and computers and telecommunications are central to the working of modern banks, building societies, finance houses and such. It is not only bar coding, credit cards and electronic funds-transfer in shops that are making life easier for customers as far as handling money is concerned. A large proportion of money transfer between organisations is electronic now. Firms in the world of finance have as much need for word-processor operators and data-preparation staff as those in commerce. Here, too, there are many openings for school and college leavers with few qualifications; some knowledge of accounting and/or economics will certainly help, however. Again promotion into supervisory roles, management and computer operations can be rapid.

CASE STUDY

Roger is in his early forties and a year ago succeeded at interview to become the manager of a large electronic office. The company is a large finance house, with many kinds of dealings that depend on word processing, database management, sophisticated accounting and financial software, and highly reliable telecommunications links with the branches.

He started his career with the equivalent of a BTEC Higher National Certificate in Commerce (this was nearly 20 years ago). He joined a small local business as accounts clerk but found this didn't stretch him enough. Indeed, he was not really happy in any of his first few jobs, although looking back he agrees that they all gave him valuable experience.

One of these jobs was as a trainee computer operator with a bank. He found it hard to get excited about that work too, but at least it opened his eyes to the possibilities of IT. The bank put him in touch with one of their customers, a travel agency with several branches. This was just at the time when microcomputers, Prestel and computerised databases were reaching more progressive firms. Roger was appointed to set up such new systems here.

At last Roger felt stretched! The work was varied and always interesting and he was able to make decisions and see them through. On the wave of IT the agency became successful spectacularly and he found himself in the position of receiving tempting offers from other companies. He accepted one and repeated his success (and his enjoyment) with a national firm of car spare-part suppliers. Roger could now afford to develop his knowledge by studying at home and going on lots of short training courses (many of which the agency paid for). His new employers are happy to leave him to run all their office facilities, though his job description is actually rather vague. He has a large team of assistant managers and sees his role as ensuring they all work together effectively while he explores new possibilities for the improvement of atmosphere and efficiency.

Conclusions

All companies and organisations have offices; all offices handle large volumes of information. IT is central to their work. This is just as true of commerce and banking as of offices in the more common sense.

Work in all these at all levels shows steady long-term growth, while there are plenty of opportunities of entry, however few or many your qualifications. Graduates, especially in business-related subjects, economics and computing can enter a broad range of management and development careers. On the other hand, there are plenty of openings for school and college leavers with or without qualifications in English, typing, commerce or office practice.

Salaries

Early 1987 salary ranges were:
Data preparation: £4500–£10,500
Data preparation management: £7000–£20,000
Word processing: £5000–£12,000
Management: £12,000–£30,000.

This is the first time that an idea of the salary ranges you can expect in computing work has been set down in this book. There are some important points to make in this context, however; they apply throughout the book. Firstly, note that the values are for early 1987, when this book went to press. Throughout the industry, wages and salaries are rising faster than in many other areas, and certainly faster than the rate of inflation. This is mainly because there is a significant shortage of the knowledge and skills concerned. It is also the case that most companies involved are successful; they are growing fast and so are their profits and as a result they can afford to pay more.

These two factors, allied with the shortage of good training schemes throughout the industry, mean too that companies often will pay new staff a joining bonus (a 'golden hallo'), give their employees extra benefits as well as a wage or salary and offer promotion when they start to think of leaving.

For all these reasons, the salaries given in this book should be taken with a fairly large pinch of salt. The only way you can get a true picture of what people in this industry are paid is to study lots of advertisements and talk to lots of recruitment agencies (and then you must accept that what you find out will quickly go out of date). The 'Big Bang' of the Stock Exchange at the end of 1986 tended to push pay up temporarily; already some surveys are showing that rises are falling below the national norms.

It is also important for you to bear in mind that pay varies greatly from one part of the country to another. (So do the costs of living of course.) The best rates are found in the south east, especially in London, and in Britain's silicon valleys, along the M4 from London to past Bristol, and in patches elsewhere. Pay varies too with the size of the firm, with smaller companies tending to pay more, at the lower levels at least, than the larger ones.

What about those benefits ('perks')? Again, much depends on time, place and size of company, but most IT staff will get more from their employers than a monthly cheque. End of year bonuses are very common, adding perhaps 5 per cent to the salary of people on the lowest scales and maybe twice that at the top. Some quarter of the workforce have share option schemes available, with twice as many getting medical insurance. Company cars are becoming common bait as well, with 75 per cent of senior staff getting them and 10 per cent of people in the middle levels; even some public employers are offering cars to computing staff now. Other perks in the market include free pension schemes and lunches, and cheap loans and mortgages. Often none of these things is mentioned in advertisements, but it is not wise to ask about them too openly.

Chapter 4

In the Computer Department

Background

Although the computers of today are far more reliable and can do things automatically much more than those a decade ago, the largest ones need a lot of staff to keep them working efficiently. Examples are the machines in such organisations as a regional gas-board headquarters with more than a million records of information to handle (for more than a million customers). The central computer department will also have to handle all kinds of other work. This will include keeping up to date information of the whole system including very detailed maps of every street and road (for planning and maintenance, and for use in emergencies). They will include the personnel and salary records of thousands of staff, the very complex accounts of such a large organisation and all kinds of other administrative material.

Systems in the smaller offices require little attention nowadays, however. The word processing, accounting and general management functions, as well as the telecommunications links, are handled by separate individual microcomputers; it is, however, becoming more common for those to be linked together into a so-called local area network, as we have seen. This means that particularly costly peripherals, the high-capacity storage drives and high-speed printers can be shared; it also means that information can be shared even more easily. (On the other hand, it can happen that if one part of a network breaks down, the whole system cannot be used.) None of these systems requires much in the way of special computing staff.

It is quite possible that the huge computing systems could become as reliable and automatic as the smaller ones are. After all, the cheap microcomputers that are so common today in homes, schools and offices are much more powerful than the world's biggest machines years back, yet they are extremely reliable and are easy for the user alone to run.

However, at the moment, many thousands of people are employed in those large computer departments. It is not likely that the need for them will disappear entirely in your working life. After all, as those big systems shrink to automatic filing-cabinet-size machines, companies and government organisations will be starting to use other big ones thousands of times more powerful.

Data Control

The data-control staff have a crucial function in linking the data-preparation department (Chapter 3) and the computer room itself. It is important to realise that a large computer system may cost far in excess of £1 million. To make the purchase really worthwhile, it must be in use as much as possible. This means that shift work is common in computer operations; it also involves on-site maintenance and repair staff.

It is the task of the data-control manager and the other staff in the department to ensure a steady flow of information into and out of the computer. In other words, they must schedule the demands on the system, decide priorities and ensure continuous smooth working at the most efficient level. The data controllers must also ensure that the information comes in in a suitable form and may need to advise management about these aspects of each new task the system has to handle.

Scheduling the output is just as important. It is no good printing out statistical reports at several pages a second if the printout is left lying around for days: it must be checked at once and then passed straight to the person who needs it.

Another responsibility commonly given to the data-control department is control of the stock of consumables needed by the computer system. Although this will not often include spare parts (that needs more specialist knowledge), you can imagine how much paper is needed by printers that print several pages a second or produce many thousands of letters or bills every single day. Guess how people will feel if you run out; guess how much it will cost the organisation to close down the computer even for just a few days.

After consideration of the importance of data control, it may be surprising that often it is a job undertaken by school or college leavers with few qualifications. The skills needed are, however, to be able to work under pressure and often in unsocial hours. The work is much more interesting, and more demanding, than data preparation; it tends to be better paid and offers much the same promotion prospects if you are suitable. The obvious first steps up are, however, toward running the data-control department. If you can keep neat systematic records of work done, those steps up will be a lot easier. By the time you reach that responsible position of data controller you will realise that the job title should really be temper controller. You will find that almost daily you are in the middle of conflicts between users (the data-preparation department or someone in management wanting something fast) and the computer operators who feel the pressure is becoming too great. You can be sure that it is you who will be blamed for errors or for jobs being finished behind time.

When things like that happen, the data controller must find out the real causes of the problem, then try to devise systems that will prevent the trouble recurring. You will need to be ready then to argue your case with management if you decide that major changes are needed or that more money must be spent.

All the same, you will see by now that this is important and exciting work (and therefore well paid). You will learn a great deal about computer operation. Thus if your real ambition is to get into work in the computer room, you'll find that going into data control (directly or through data preparation) will provide a sensible route. All this is true too of data control in the large commercial or public organisation; it is also true in the much rarer computer bureau (see Chapter 6 for more on that).

CASE STUDY

Maria, aged 23 years, has just succeeded in escaping (as she puts it) from an insurance company's data-preparation department into data control. She has found that she has replaced boredom with hassle. Before the move she never felt her work was real; now she doesn't seem to have time to think, let alone relax. Also, whereas in her former job Maria was one of many, now she is just a dogsbody, at the beck and call of all, needed for hundreds of jobs an hour.

That's all true, but it's also the truth that Maria loves every minute of her new job. She is learning at a huge rate. What she is learning is not just about working with the computer systems: she is also finding out more about data preparation than she could have dreamed while she was working there. Much of her time is still in data preparation, of course, for she is involved in assisting liaison between that department and the computer staff. It gives her a funny feeling though, to be bringing messages and instructions to the people who used to watch over her work.

All the same, perhaps she enjoys learning about the computers most. This is a totally new world for her and she is happy to do all sorts of odd jobs for the staff there, all of whom she finds friendly and cheerful. The data-control staff with whom she is officially based are friendly and cheerful too. Maria finds that rather hard to believe, in view of the huge pressures they so often seem to work under. She feels that she is busy, but looking at them makes her rather humble.

Clearly, Maria realises that data control is important as well as exciting. She hopes that she will be able to get promotion in her new department, but she isn't quite sure whether she'll be able to be as friendly and cheerful as the people she now works for. Maria seems surprisingly settled; fair enough, of course, in view of the fact that she has a home and family to work for as well. One can see her moving to another company in a few years, after getting a few steps of the promotion she deserves. Maybe she'll end up in charge of a large data-preparation department or she could get happily into librarianship.

Data Library

One big reason that computer departments need so many staff is that it is impossible to keep the thousands of discs (or tapes) that carry the millions of records all on line to the central processor at once. Not only would it be out of the question to buy and maintain thousands of disc (or tape) drives, but no computer of today could work with so many. Even if the computer room contains a couple of hundred drive units (and even that many is rare) you can see that at any time the large majority of records and programs will not be in use.

It is the role of the data librarians to store all those discs (or tapes) safe yet ready for immediate access. The biggest computer departments will have data libraries larger than most branch book libraries, and more staff. (In the smaller installations, of course, the data-control people will look after the few hundred discs.)

In many ways the work of data librarians is more demanding than that of book librarians, but fewer qualifications are needed. For sure, some skills are much the same: neatness, the ability to work under pressure, being able to keep good records and always up to date. That's because some tasks are much the same: addition of new stock and deletion of stock no longer needed, monitoring issues and returns, knowledge of where anything is at any time, sudden emergency demands dealt with quietly and efficiently.

In addition, though, there are special aspects of looking after computer data. In particular, various security demands must be met. Computer data are often irreplaceable; it is the data librarian's job to ensure that back-up copies are made, and looked after, of the important data discs. Computer data are often secret; there will therefore be security precautions to maintain, including making sure that discs of confidential data are given only to those staff allowed to handle them. Fire is another possible hazard; back-up copies of the most important discs may need to be stored in a special room or even in a separate building. Finally, damage to a disc must be avoided: the data-library staff will need to inspect each one as it goes out and comes back and to ensure always that the library stock is stored properly and handled gently.

School and college leavers with good GCSE grades or equivalent find data-library work exciting and rewarding. It is also fairly easy to enter from general office work or the data-preparation department.

To head a large data library is a good aim that is not hard to achieve if you show yourself to be suitable over the years. As with data control, however, this area is a good way into computer operations. So let's take a look at that field now.

Computer Operator

As we are now talking about the running of a large computer room, it is clear that the computer operators, like the data-control staff, will need to work in shifts. Their task is to tend to the computer's needs from minute to minute, in particular to ensure that all the peripherals (input and output units and disc and/or tape drives) are working as they should be. In some computer rooms just keeping the printers supplied with paper may be a full-time job. The same may apply to the bursters and decollaters, the machines that divide the continuous paper output of the printers into sheets, separate the copies and perhaps fold and seal letters and invoices ready for mailing.

More interesting work at this level involves tending of the disc drives. There is a steady flow of discs between the library and the computer room as different programs are run and/or different parts of the largest files are worked with. The right discs will need to be got from the library at the right time, put on the right drives at the right time and returned after the job is finished. That work is not difficult. The author of each program used will ensure that messages are output at the console, as the main control desk is called, to say what to do and when. Also, each job that has to be run will come with clear instructions. Errors can occur of course; the computer operators must know how to recognise these and what is the correct action to take. (The action may be to call in a programmer or an engineer.) Normally, it is the task of the chief operator to run everything from the console. At the start of each job the right commands are input to the computer and then, as the job proceeds, the computer will output requests. However, even in quite large installations, there will be only one chief operator. Each shift that he or she is not on duty needs a shift leader to run the system as just described. Shift leader is therefore the first real step up from computer operator.

The work in most computer rooms that run shifts is often arranged so that long trouble-free jobs are carried out at night. Night-shift staff may therefore have an easy time. While you may find it easy to play cards or read, this work is a golden opportunity for further study.

All the same, computer operation always involves a lot of individual responsibility. Even as a junior, you'd find that very soon you will be left to fairly complex tasks for long periods on your own. It is up to you to prove that you can carry that responsibility. That is true, even if you are the most junior operator in a large room and have little to do but keep the place and the equipment clean.

As you work your way up the operations ladder you will gain a great deal of experience. It is tempting for you to start to think about moving to programming work (Chapter 6), but a trainee or junior programmer does not earn as much as an experienced shift leader. The work of chief operator is to supervise all the above. In that post you will also have to watch over the training of your staff (and help with their personal and career problems). Again, keeping clear and precise records of work input and output is crucial, as is checking the instructions for each job before passing them to the operators. The most important task is to schedule the system properly, perhaps in co-operation with the data controller.

CASE STUDY

Sebastian in his mid-thirties reached the position of senior shift leader in the computer department of a regional electricity board headquarters. The installation is a very large one, as it needs to be with the records of several million customers to look after. Now Sebastian looks after it, at least when he is in charge of the night shift, for then the operations manager is out of the way.

Night-shift work is fairly quiet; during the day various small data-processing jobs are carried out, but a major load on the computer is handling the needs of the users of the several hundred terminals. The night shift is reserved for such peripheral intensive jobs as printing out the electricity bills, on average over a hundred thousand a week. However, even on night shift there is quite a lot for the staff to do, and the shift leader has a huge responsibility. Something can go wrong: it is the shift leader's job to try to prevent this from happening and to deal rapidly and effectively with problems that do arise.

Sebastian actually wanted to be a programmer, but he could not afford to go to university (the best place for training programmers at the time). He started work as a trainee programmer with a large supermarket chain, but found he did not progress as fast as he wanted. Therefore he transferred to operations, with the same company, and after his training period moved to the electricity board. Sometimes he wonders if he should have stayed in programming. He can see, however, that, at least in his kind of organisation, programming is not as interesting as his current job. Maybe systems analysis? After all he will be 40 years old soon and he doesn't want to get into a rut yet.

Conclusions

Many staff may work in a large computer department, in data control, in the library and in actual operations. In each area there are several steps on the ladder and you can enter at the bottom with few qualifications. No technical knowledge is needed, but to make progress it is crucial to work hard, to accept responsibility and to learn as much as you can about the whole system and its parts. Computing and IT certificates are useful, but English is once more the most useful subject.

Salaries

Early 1987 salary ranges were:

Data control: £7000–£13,000
Data control management: £10,000–£17,000
Library: £5000–£10,000
Library management: £8000–£14,000
Computer operation: £5000–£14,500
Computer operation management: £10,000–£16,000.

As you may expect for a rapidly growing and developing industry, there is a huge range of job names for workers in a data-processing installation. In this chapter the most common ones for each role discussed have been given, but you need to be aware that in each case there will be a number of alternatives. The diagram opposite shows the relations between staff in a typical medium-sized data-processing department (but in practice not only will the job titles vary from place to place, but so too will at least some of the links). Overall, however, the figure is a fair representation of typical practice. Smaller systems will require fewer staff, so that some of the layers and/or columns may disappear. In the case of larger systems, there will be more people in the lower layers especially, as well perhaps as more vertical branches.

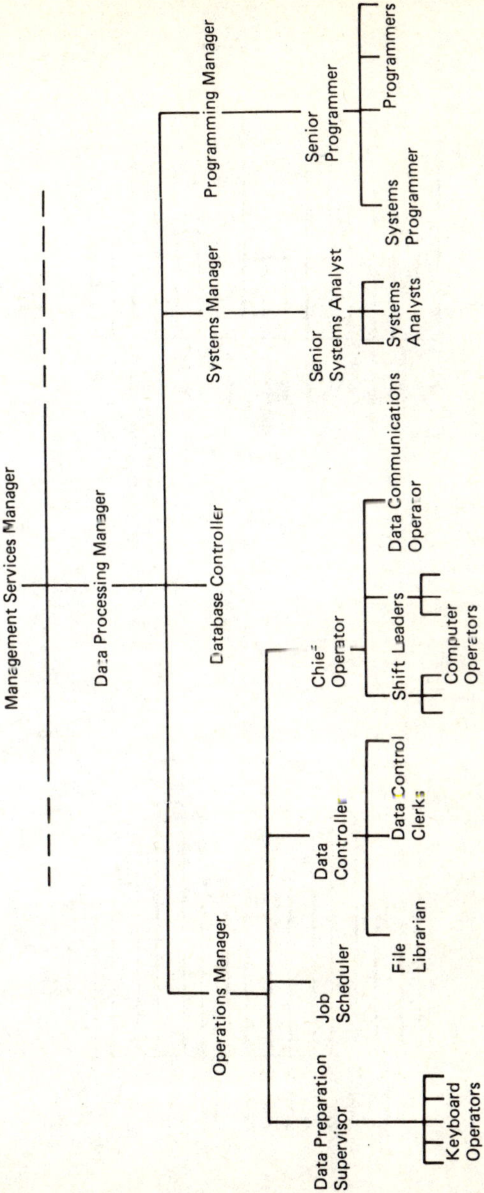
Management Services Manager
Data Processing Manager
Database Controller
Systems Manager
Programming Manager
Operations Manager
Senior Systems Analyst
Systems Analysts
Senior Programmer
Systems Programmer
Programmers
Data Preparation Supervisor
Keyboard Operators
Job Scheduler
Data Controller
File Librarian
Data Control Clerks
Chief Operator
Shift Leaders
Computer Operators
Data Communications Operator

Staffing make-up of the average UK computer installation

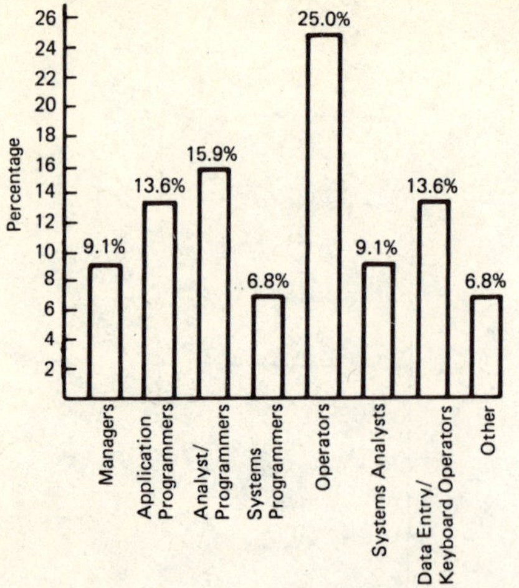

Rates of increase/decrease in employment levels

	1985-86	1986-87	1985-87
Managers	+4.6%	+2.4%	+7.1%
Systems Analysts	+10.6%	+7.0%	+18.4%
Analyst/Programmers	+2.9%	+8.3%	+11.4%
Systems Programmers	+2.1%	+6.1%	+8.4%
Application Programmers	+5.2%	+6.2%	+11.8%
Operators	+1.75%	+2.3%	+4.2%
Data Entry	+3.0%	−5.1%	−2.3%
Other	−1.6%	+1.3%	−0.0%
Total	+3.4%	+3.5%	+6.9%

Annual rate of staff turnover (1985–86)

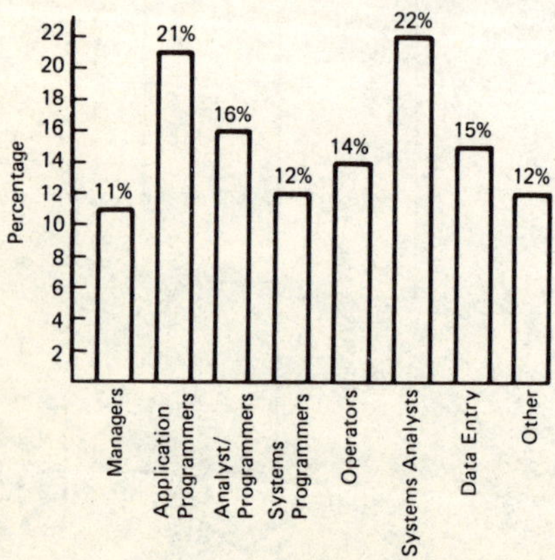

The Market

There are some rather worrying aspects of the IT industry; they may be just symptoms of a rapidly growing field, but they are worrying all the same. The picture includes severe shortages of staff in many areas at many levels and the resultant tendencies for wages and salaries to rise fast and for people to stay for fairly short periods with a given firm. You may feel that none of this should worry you as a potential employee, yet you must try to think of your long-term future and accept that greater stability would benefit everyone.

Other information relevant here is that training levels seem to be very poor generally, so that in some types of work people receive no further training for a year or more after starting with a company. This may well be a reason for the fact that in some types of work people stay with a firm for less than two years on average.

The IT industries are also marked by a large number of surveys that try to find out what is going on. It is interesting that the results of these surveys can differ greatly; sometimes they seem to show quite different trends. All the same, you may like to see some of the findings from a major survey carried out in the autumn of 1986, and draw your own conclusions.

The last worrying factor in this business is the level of 'poaching', when companies approach employees of other firms and induce them to move. It is nice to feel wanted in this way, but there are legal aspects in contract law to bear in mind. Legal or not, there have been cases where a whole department's staff has been induced to transfer to another organisation!

Chapter 5

The Professionals

Systems Analysis

To many people in the computing and IT industries, the systems analyst has the most interesting and responsible work. Certainly, a really good one can have an excellent career and be very well paid indeed for his or her trouble. The work involves a careful examination of the needs of a firm or department and an assessment of how those needs are (or are not) currently being met. Next is to design a suitable system (this need not be IT based, but normally is) to meet the present and likely future needs most effectively. Lastly, the systems analyst will probably have to supervise the introduction of the new system (that is, if management agrees to go ahead with it). Thereafter there may be an ongoing distant supervision role. Large companies are likely to have their own systems analyst; indeed, many have big systems-analysis departments. Smaller ones, on the other hand, will call in this kind of expertise when they need it. Thus many systems analysts are consultants, working on their own or in partnership in a specialist firm.

Clearly, a deep and wide knowledge and experience of the industry is required in this business. It is not therefore for the school or college leaver and even many graduates enter systems analysis only after some time finding out about the world by working in business management, computer operations or programming (Chapter 6).

CASE STUDY

Jenny works in the systems analysis department of a motor-manufacturing company. While the company is not very big, it makes great use of computers. Jenny and her colleagues have the main task of investigating and planning new uses.

Jenny is a polytechnic graduate in mechanical engineering. She did a sandwich course and during her industrial work experience she became deeply involved with robots. Now, four years after graduation, she doesn't have much to do with robots as such. Her current field of interest and, indeed, research is flexible manufacturing systems. These certainly involve robots in production and assembly, but more important is the attempt to automate the whole process of design and manufacture.

With a colleague Jenny forms a little team working full-time in this field. At the moment the two of them are looking at flexible manufacturing systems in various industries around the world. They have to do a lot of travel, research into patents, and talk to engineers of all kinds, to evaluate possibly relevant new ideas.

The work is urgent, though: Jenny and her team mate must present a full report to the senior systems analysts within three months. Jenny thinks they can do it; moreover, she believes they will come up with important and feasible plans. If they succeed, Jenny expects to get promotion to head a larger team. If they fail, she is certain that she can gain the same rewards by moving to a different company. What of 10 or 15 years' time? Jenny is clear about that: she plans to be leading her own successful consultancy in fully automated factory systems.

For a given job the systems analyst starts with a feasibility study. This means looking in detail at the work being done and the method by which it is done. Often, however, a new system is needed for some procedure that does not yet exist: for instance, a firm selling for cash may now decide to sell also by mail order. In this case the analyst will speak to the people who are organising the change and try to find out what they want to achieve, contributing from personal experience of similar jobs done before.

The analyst must chat with users, perhaps even customers too, to find out what they want from any new system. This crucial part of the job, the recording and collection of initial facts, requires the ability to get on well with people and a 'Sherlock Holmes' ability to nose out people's ideas, opinions and fears. The next step, once the facts have been collected and sorted out, is to analyse the situation. To do this the analyst may set the facts out in a graphic (flow chart) form. A picture tends to be easier to analyse than a lot of text and you can get more in symbol form on a page than in words. The analyst will then check again with management. Once the users have agreed what information will be coming in and what they will expect to be output, the analyst will define the system: the processes to do the job.

Now is the stage at which the analyst looks at different ways of meeting the needs found. Now is the stage where various solutions that involve IT, as well as others which do not, are compared. If the best solution found does not involve IT, then the rest of the analyst's work on that job is not relevant here, so let us assume that it does.

This stage of systems analysis involves working out the best solution. How can IT help? What are the computing needs? How should the computer(s) link into a local network or with systems elsewhere? What programs will do the job? How much should systems that the firm or department already has be used?

If software exists that can do the needed work exactly, or nearly exactly, then this will help to determine what central processor should be brought in. (No software runs on all computers; the current major problems of incompatability will remain into the next century.)

If no current software fits the user's needs fully, the analyst will call on a programmer (Chapter 6) to tailor something suitable, or even invite a programming team to design software from scratch. (A big company with its own systems analyst(s) will likely have that expertise available too.) Whether that is the case, or not, the analyst will need to check that management approves this next step; it will not be cheap. Then the analyst will draw a broad flow chart for the programmer(s) with details of files and input and output. The programmer and analyst will discuss the chart and the details and when they are agreed the programmer can get on with this part of the job.

In designing a system the analyst will always have kept in mind the following points:

1. Who are the users and therefore how simple can we make the system?
2. How easy is it to get the information we require from the system?
3. How many different jobs can we do without complicating the system too much?

While all this time the analyst will have kept management informed of progress, when the system has been chosen it is time to get full approval to go ahead with purchase (or rental) and installation. It may well be that management is unclear about computer operations, or even fears modern technology. The analyst therefore will need to be able to write good clear (and short!) reports and be prepared to discuss them fully. Detailed costings are essential here.

Once the system to be brought in, and the software work already mentioned, are approved the analyst must schedule its introduction. This may need close work with architects, builders and designers. Certainly, it will need close work with all the people concerned with usage, and that includes the cleaning, security and catering staff.

At the same time the analyst will prepare detailed documentation. Here the ability to communicate effectively is most important, for the documentation is for a lower-level staff, namely the ones discussed in the last two chapters. Previously, the analyst was communicating mainly with management and with other professionals, but he or she should be able to speak everybody's language.

It is also the analyst's responsibility to prepare detailed test data to check out the completed system and to arrange the tests. Once this is done it is time to prepare a final schedule to put the new system into full operation and to assist the users to prepare for the new system. You'll even have to make sure that the new forms are ready and any other changes are made. During the actual implementation of the new computer system, the systems analyst is like Father Christmas: being expected to deal at once with anything that goes wrong, no matter how small. Other duties that systems analysts may be expected to do are training the users in their work with the new system, running the system for a specific period of time and being on call after that in case further problems arise.

Systems analysts may find employment in almost any of the areas in the computer world: working for firms who use computers a lot, for a computer bureau which does tasks for a variety of customers (Chapter 6), or perhaps for a software house whose function is to supply the services of analysts and programmers. Also, many act as freelance consultants. The in-house analysts have a limited scope once all the systems are computerised. As a result they tend to move from job to job. They may also act as senior programmers in these places. There is great scope to learn the role of systems analysis in private companies. A computer bureau may have attached to it a software house which supplies the systems analysis expertise. Here the variety of work is virtually unlimited and very interesting. For programmers moving into the job of analyst this could be a good place to get experience, for they would be able to call on the varied knowledge of a large group of analysts. Note, however, that software houses and consultants usually take only experienced analysts and in many instances promote promising programmers. The freelance systems analyst sells his or her services either as an analyst or as a programmer. If the client requires both, a freelance programmer may be called in to work as a partner for that task.

Much experience of the industry is needed by the successful systems analyst. There is a great shortage in the field (and this will remain for a decade or two yet); even so, it is rare for a school or college leaver to work up through computer operations or programming to this kind of work. The normal way in is for graduates, or at least for people with good grades at A level or in the higher levels of BTEC; the most suitable subjects for study are those related to office or business management, economics, accountancy and such, rather than computer science alone. The systems analyst should also be able to answer 'yes' to each of the following questions.

1. Are you imaginative? Your main function is creating a working system from facts gathered within the scope of the job in the organisation, so you must be able to gather facts effectively.

2. Are you a good listener? If you cannot listen you won't hear what the user wants the computer to do or what is happening now. It is important to know what is happening now to be able to build up the right system (or a better one). If you don't know how to listen you won't know how to ask the right questions to get the facts. (Try testing your own listening ability by taping a talk or discussion from the radio or TV and then see how much of it you can repeat or discuss intelligently. At first it will only be the first five or ten minutes.)
3. Have you the ability to communicate effectively, both verbally and in writing? As an analyst your first duty is to tell the users how you interpret their present procedure; only second is how you will make it work using a computer system or how you would change the organisation so that it works better on the computer than previously. This is where communication comes into its own. As a systems analyst you must also be able to communicate ideas to the programmer accurately, so that good software can be written with the least possible difficulty.
4. Can you sell yourself and your ideas? You must be clear and persuasive, but not pigheaded. If you believe your ideas are right and good for the job in mind, you must not be swayed by a strong-willed user, but if the user points out real weaknesses you should be prepared to change your mind. The building or planning of a system is a team effort, not a systems analyst's sole right.
5. Are you patient and tactful?
6. Have you an eye for detail and an aptitude with numbers?

CASE STUDY

Adrian says 'I am actually called an information technologist, but so far I've mainly been in programming and systems analysis.' He graduated in mathematics a couple of years ago, from such a traditional university that he did absolutely no computing in his course. He works in the large information technology department of a chemicals company, and spent his first six months becoming thoroughly expert in the programming language PL1. He received quite a lot of actual training but reckoned he learned most by 'sitting by Nellie', working with experienced people, in other words.

The team of programmers and analysts with which Adrian spends most of his time have been developing a series of packages for controlling the company's industrial processes. The task involves more than control, for there is a modelling component with which managers can plan the processes and work out costs and so on.

The company's information technologists may be called on to work on new products (systems and software) in any department. The departments include customer relations, stock, accounting, personnel, marketing, research and development, as well as engineering and the general offices. While over half of the information technologists are graduates, few have been through initial training or education in anything to do with IT. A lot are, naturally, scientists and engineers, but there are a couple of historians, several people with accountancy or management training and even a classics graduate. The company has a policy that all new professional staff spend time in each of the departments. Adrian liked that very much; not only did it enable him to meet people, but he could learn the basics of the company's business and structure quickly.

He enjoys mathematics, so would like to specialise in work such as accounting or research. Whether he will stay with the same company is not certain: he likes it a lot and is well treated, but he feels that he would like to find out about other industries before settling down too much.

The long description may make it sound as if systems analysis requires superhuman skills. In practice, of course, a large project will be handled by a team, perhaps quite a big one, working closely with management. However, management have their own problems and often an O & M (organisation and methods) analyst (or more than one) will go in between. In any event O & M staff can much help with the less demanding parts of the systems analyst's work.

O & M

Not all companies employ organisation and methods (O & M) personnel and not all O & M people are connected with computers directly or even indirectly. All the same, no book on computer personnel would be complete without a mention of them. The work does not require any technical computer knowledge, so is a career which school-leavers may well enter into at junior or trainee level. The job is very similar to that of the systems analyst, but needs no technical ability: a project is handed over to a systems analyst once it has been studied and analysed by the O & M officer concerned. This person therefore still needs most of the skills of the systems analyst; many come with time and experience.

The O & M analyst applies common sense to business problems. All O & M solutions are the application of common sense, so you may ask why we need specialists to do this. The answer is simple. The managers are applying their time and brainpower to their various fields: the accountant and how to keep cash flowing, the factory manager and how to keep the production lines moving, and so on. The O & M person works full-time looking at how things are done and improving the procedure by common-sense ideas.

The role of O & M and systems analysts would start when they get together with their respective managers, and the manager of the department to be studied, to discuss the problems as each sees them. For the sake of an example assume the accountant has asked for assistance in the collection and recording of cash received through the post and production of monthly sales statistics. The areas to be studied will be agreed and the length of time required for the study is estimated. The O & M officer and the systems analyst will agree at what stage the computer people will or may be brought in. The O & M analyst will then start the investigation, either working alone or as part of a team.

The first area of study here is the postal section where the mail comes in. The personnel who open the mail need to be questioned with care, so that information about volumes and procedures can be collected; you will also need to examine and think about the layout of the post room. After the O & M analyst has studied the various departments concerned and discussed the problems as seen by the accountant it is time to sit down and analyse the problem. He or she will ask the same basic questions as the systems analyst: when, where, what, who, how and why? If the job seems suited to computerisation possible ideas are then discussed with the systems analyst. Some may be changed to make the change-over cheaper or easier.

The O & M officer and systems analyst will talk next with the accountants and the accountancy department staff to find out what sort of reports they require and how frequently they should be produced. From previous experience O & M analysts may be able to suggest how to make reports more meaningful or easier to use. The systems analyst may offer suggestions based on technical know-how, such as asking if the accountants would like graphs. Between them, they will agree the final reports. After that the O & M analyst will draw up a detailed specification of what is required and where the input will come from. This is handed to the systems analyst after it has been agreed by all concerned.

Once the system is installed and tested and the program is written, tested and working, the O & M analyst takes over again. The task now is to ensure that information is moving correctly between departments, that staff are doing things correctly and that the results are satisfactory.

It can be seen that O & M work is important; it is also very interesting. Many systems analysts start in this field. There is lots of scope for junior O & M analysts as experience is the best teacher here and to start at the bottom of the O & M ladder, as long as you receive formal training as well, is the best you can do.

There are many techniques which O & M staff learn in their career. These include such things as forms design. This is a grossly underrated job, as a well-designed form can save a lot of valuable time. Another technique that the O & M person will learn is office layout. This can be extremely important, for it is crucial that paper flows smoothly and quickly through the system and reaches the data-preparation department as soon as possible. The measurement of clerical work is another O & M technique. It is important, first, to be able to assess what actual savings in personnel can be achieved by computerisation and, second, what volume can be handled by the data-preparation staff so that enough keyboards are available to do the required work. The ability to measure clerical work accurately can be the deciding factor in whether or not to computerise a particular job.

Once the job has been programmed and tested and is ready to run, the O & M department will be called in to implement the new procedure. This means writing clear and detailed instructions for the users, including what to do in case of errors and how to balance the various reports produced by the computer. An important part of this implementation stage is the training of the staff in the new system and how to use it properly.

From the above it can be seen that the task of an O & M analyst is a very demanding one. The O & M analyst may find employment in larger private or public organisations. After extensive experience is gained, the next step is to find employment with certain types of consultants or O & M contract houses: organisations that hire out O & M personnel on a time or project basis.

Freelance Work

There are opportunities in IT-related work for people who want to go on their own rather than be employed. Consultants in other fields (such as marketing, public relations, safety, staff recruitment and office design) who may specialise in working for computer and IT companies are not included; their work is covered by other titles in the present series.

In this business few people actually do go on their own right from the start of leaving full-time education or training. More than in many fields, working in IT requires experience. Not only do you need to know the industry, but you need to know how to find work, how to rate your financial worth and how to run a small business. That may not all apply to data preparation and such work as market research. However, you should be aware that people doing work in these areas from home quite often find they are badly oppressed. You may be disabled or cannot take full-time work because of family reasons, but even if you have few qualifications, be on the lookout for sharks!

If you have the right qualifications for word processing (Chapter 3) and cannot work full-time, discuss your case with one of the large secretarial agencies (or your local ones if any). Part-time, holiday and short-period work is fairly easy to get (especially as your experience grows); most agencies also keep details of jobs that can be done at home. In that context, note that if you can afford your own word-processing system (costing from about £300) you will be able to do this kind of work for students, authors and local small firms. Advertise your availability in local supermarkets and corner shops, and in universities and colleges, and try the managers of as many nearby shops and offices as you can stand! *Running Your Own Typing Service*, published by Kogan Page, provides much useful information.

Many people have tried to set up their own businesses selling hardware (very expensive) or software (quite expensive). Very few remain in business long. Apart from the expense of getting stock, to rent a decent shop is not cheap (and to sell from home is rarely likely to lead to success, even if by mail order). Advertising and the costs of selling (including post and phone), as well as the need for product maintenance, must be allowed for in your costings.

Freelance programmers, systems analysts and technical authors can often do much better. This is because there are fewer overheads and working from home need present no problem as long as you have a corner and any necessary computer hardware and telephone equipment. The biggest competition is from others doing the same while staying in full-time work: you can beat them in your dealings with customers, but they are in a better financial position. Much the same applies to the range of freelance consultancy work. The range is very large – from small business systems for corner shops and word processors for offices to communications, computer-aided design and manufacture and company organisation. Most consultant firms also tend to specialise in certain areas of business activity, such as forestry, catering, travel or public administration.

Wide experience is certainly of value in all these areas of professional freelance activity, but if you have that experience, a lot of drive and fire, and a real need or desire for home-based work, you can succeed. After all, most people in IT agree that the next few decades will see a fast-growing number of home-based self-employed workers.

Fees are generally quoted on a daily basis, though clients may also be expected to cover travelling and incidental expenses. The range of fees is enormous: from £60 a day for the very cheapest programmers (and truly that is far too cheap) to figures in the £1000 per day range for top consultants and systems analysts. Don't sell yourself short is good advice. You must never forget that there will be days, perhaps many of them, when you have no work; the fees you charge must cover slow periods as well as all your overheads. Note too that a freelancer may well not be expected to charge for the initial discussion meetings, even if those don't lead to a contract.

Why should a company decide to use a freelance specialist rather than its own staff? It is worth looking briefly at the reasons, for, after all, maybe one day you will be such a freelancer and have to persuade companies to give you contracts.

The word 'contract' gives one clue. A freelance consultant will have a specific job to do and he or she will not be able to leave until that task is completed to the client's satisfaction. On the other hand, as we have seen, there is a rapid turnover of employed staff, so there is no guarantee that in-house staff will stay on until the end of a project.

The use of freelance staff can be very cost-effective too, even though the hourly or daily rate may seem high. The client will pay just for the time put in on the job in question and when the job is finished will not have to go on giving a salary to someone with little work to do. Many other costs are reduced by this approach too. Thus advertising, interviewing and other recruitment expenses are much lower, as are those of taxation, insurance and pensions. There will be less to spend on office space, equipment and other overheads, while the freelance person cannot expect holiday and sick pay.

All this applies at least as much to the final main area of freelance work: hardware maintenance and repairs. Like car maintenance and repairs, this requires much experience and a lot of money spent on tools, manuals, test equipment and spare parts. Unlike the case of cars, there is a desperate shortage (at the moment) of such services, and some quite large maintenance companies have grown fast from a one-person operation. Maintenance is an important area and more is said about it in the *Specialist Organisations* section of the next chapter.

CASE STUDY

Alice is 38 years old. She trained as a primary-school teacher and spent ten years in schools before she started to feel that she could put her skills to better use in industry. One summer holiday she was able to get a six-week period with a software house; she found that the life and the work fascinated her and resigned from teaching after less than a month had gone by. She was able to stay with the software house which was at the time dabbling with home-learning software for cheap microcomputers.

The company's main work was for the insurance industry. As well as contributing a lot to the home-learning programme, Alice worked hard at understanding the big ICL mainframe computer and programming it. She found a major frustration, though. Although the software house sent her on several training courses and her busy colleagues were always helpful, she felt that she did not learn as fast as she could.

A year or so later it happened that the software house ran into a long quiet patch. The home-learning scheme had been a failure and, although the insurance software went on selling well, there was a lot less new work to do. This was Alice's chance. She spoke to the managing director about her dream to provide really well-designed training courses. He made some inquiries around town and found that if they put on some courses there would be plenty of people wanting to join them. Alice was given the rush job of designing two courses to be run on the company's premises a month later and everyone, including Alice, was amazed at their success.

When the software house's business picked up again, Alice decided to leave and start up her own training business. She came to an agreement with the managing director that she could arrange courses using the ICL equipment in exchange for letting her old company have two free places on each one. Now, two years later, the arrangement works fine. Each month Alice puts on several one-day courses and one lasting two days, and she is almost always able to reach her target of 12 'students'. The rest of the month is spent on course design, preparation of materials and phoning potential clients. All this she does from home, so her overheads are very low.

She now plans to employ another teacher who would gradually take over presenting the courses; she hopes within a year to start exactly the same scheme in another big city up the motorway. Then she'll be able to buy the Jaguar car she's always wanted and drive smartly into the playground of the last school she taught at.

Teaching

Without teachers and trainers there would be no computer industry. Indeed, there would be no industry of any kind. As you climb any of a number of the ladders described in this book, you will find that you have a growing role in the training of the people that follow behind you. Most large companies have their own training departments and if you like this kind of work you should think of moving into that direction. Training is often tied in with personnel work, however, and quite different skills are involved there.

An alternative is to move into teaching in a school or college. If you have gone more than a couple of steps up your computing industry ladder already you are likely to find, however, that this means a drop in salary. That is so, even if you follow a year's training in your new profession. All the same, the hours are rather shorter (but harder) than you'll have been used to, and the holidays are longer on the whole.

A move into IT teaching or training in school or college is particularly tempting if you want part-time employment or if you want full-time employment after a period away from it. There is a shortage in all areas, but it is likely that a degree will be needed if you move straight into teaching, especially in schools.

Conclusions

Apart from a career in word processing, there is no field of work here that can reasonably be taken up part-time or self-employed without a lot of experience and significant initial financial outlay; then freelancing as a programmer or systems analyst is likely to be the most successful.

Systems analysis probably offers the most glamour in this business. The work is hard and varied, but it is exciting and can lead to very high rewards. Many systems analysts start work, at graduate level or equivalent, in large companies; many of these stay there and progress to management. O & M staff may help. Teaching is also best seen as a graduate-level profession, though mature applicants with lower qualifications but relevant experience may be able to start with part-time teaching. Training, in-house or freelance, is more likely to suit most people with experience in IT-related work, however.

Salaries

Early 1987 salary ranges were:

Systems analysis: £10,000–£50,000
O & M: £8000–£16,000
Training: £9000–£17,000
Teaching (schools): £8000–£15,000
(further education): £11,000–£16,000
(higher education): £13,000–£21,000.

Chapter 6

In the Computer Industry

Programming

By far the largest numbers of programmers are employed rather than freelance. They work with systems analysis specialists, computer bureaux and software houses and with program publishers. Freelance programmers may be able to obtain occasional contracts on part-time work with any of these but, unless this is at junior level, experience in the business is needed.

It is true that a number of small businesses have gone over to the use of computers with a cheap system and with software written for a fee by students and other inexperienced freelance people. However, this opening will become smaller as managers become wiser about standards. It is, however, the case that a small but lucrative market remains for such people to write games software for home machines. If you are really good at this, it is still possible to make a lot of money from home in this kind of work, but you need to be really good.

A program is an ordered sequence of instructions for a computer system to carry out a defined task. (The task is defined by the market, with or without the aid of systems analysts.) A programmer's work is therefore to understand the user's needs and to produce an efficient program, or suite of programs, to meet them. In the school, college or home-computing world, BASIC is the most common programming language. However, in business COBOL is still very popular, while many other languages are used for special purposes. Low-level language programs are common too, mainly for work with robots and other systems needing speed and low memory usage.

The in-house programmer or the one who works for a private

user will not have as great a variety of work as the programmers employed by a software house. The task is to write programs and suites as new jobs are put on to the computer or old ones are changed radically. The biggest in-house role, however, is likely to be maintenance of existing programs: as jobs are changed or extended the programmer will make necessary changes to existing programs. This sort of work suits experienced programmers, whereas for people who wish to move toward systems analysis this is a good place to widen experience.

The computer-bureau programmer will have a far greater variety of work. This is because the bureau will have contracts with organisations as different as chalk and cheese. Also, there will be a certain amount of opportunity to do systems analysis work, especially with the smaller contracts. Software houses offer probably the greatest variety: they employ junior as well as senior programmers, so are good places for trainee programmers to get good practical experience. They are also useful for experienced programmers to gain further experience in more advanced programming techniques.

Systems analysis and consultancy are two areas in which you cannot really freelance without a fair amount of experience, as most consulting firms only employ experienced programmers. Both these jobs are, of course, very well paid, but tend to carry a high-risk element in that no work may be available.

CASE STUDY

Stephen has been a programmer almost as long as he can remember. He got a Sinclair ZX81 home computer when he was a sixth-former and taught himself to write games. The games got better and better and he sold a number of them to various magazines. He left the sixth form early and went to a local college of further education to follow a wide ranging but thorough business programming course. He still has dreams of becoming a games software millionaire but the dreams didn't stop him working toward a more conventional career.

He did well in most aspects of his course and then joined the programming department of a computer bureau. As the bureau did not specialise in a narrow sector of industry Stephen was able to pick up a lot about the workings of many different companies. He has every intention of moving into systems analysis or program consultancy later on and feels that his experience is ideal for that.

Early last year the computer bureau decided not to stay in the same premises but to move to a smaller suite of rooms in the central business district. A number of the staff, including Stephen and the other programmers, were invited to work from home using a terminal. Stephen didn't hesitate to accept this offer. He had just married (a woman in data control, actually), and they had bought a small semi-detached house three miles from the city centre. It was no trouble to set the spare bedroom up as an office; the terminal and associated equipment does not take up much space and Stephen built a work unit with plenty of storage space to keep everything to hand. The company paid for all that, as well as having the extra phone line installed and supplying the equipment. They also pay Stephen an allowance for the use of the room and he remains a fully salaried member of staff with the usual holidays and insurance and pension cover. However, he now has the freedom to work as and when he likes. Each evening he uses the terminal to collect messages and instructions from the office, but otherwise is contracted to do 30 hours' work a week with hardly any restriction. He can go to play squash or do some gardening when he likes; he does most of the housework and will be able to look after their children later; he can take a day out in London and so on. To Stephen, however, a major advantage of this way of working is that he can also use the system for freelance work. His terminal and modem can communicate directly with systems other than that of his software house and his firm does not discourage him from networking on his own.

Sometimes Stephen still gets the urge to write a game on his home computer, but he is determined to extend his freelance programming so that as soon as possible he and his wife can set up their own business at home.

Once the overall input, output and filing demands of the program have been defined, the programmer's work breaks down into various stages. In large programming departments, each area will be the responsibility of one or more members of a team. Indeed, for really large software projects there will be a high level of specialisation. Each team is headed by a project leader working perhaps through one or more senior programmers. The project leader will have the major responsibilities of scheduling overall progress and of working with the systems analysts concerned and/or with management. A senior programmer provides the links between the project leader and the team members and their work and will be responsible for the overall control of the particular task in hand. In a large department a senior programmer will look after a number of programmers, juniors and trainees so may have little time for any actual programming most days. However, where individuals are working on their own sections or modules within a large program or suite, the senior programmer(s) and/or project leader have the major role of ensuring that the parts do not clash and that they will link neatly and efficiently into the whole.

After the initial stages of program definition have been done, mainly the task of systems analyst and team leader, work proceeds as follows, in the hands of programmers.

1. Plan how the program is to work, producing an algorithm (a statement of the steps to be followed in order). The algorithm may be in plain language or pseudo-code, or it may be in graphic form, as a flow chart or structure diagram.
2. Repeat this process on each of the parts of the algorithm (opening, input, storage, process, output, ending) in more and more detail. Eventually, the program is defined in depth as a large number of separate subsections.
3. Code each subsection, that is convert it into program statements in the chosen language and form. Coding is a logical process and needs you to keep careful paper records and to include comments within the program.
4. Start a carefully designed process of testing, making sure that each subsection (now called procedure, module or subroutine) works properly on its own. Correct errors (bugs) found, and repeat until the code is as perfect as can be. Ensure here too (as appropriate for the procedure's function) that running is as fast as possible and that the operation is user friendly. (This last means that if the module involves interaction with the user, that user will always be able to know what do do.)
5. Link the modules together in a carefully planned way, checking for and getting rid of clashes.
6. Test the whole program as above.

7. Develop and test the documentation for the users, the manuals and other instructions that the system operators and the management will need.
8. Deliver and demonstrate the package to the systems analyst or client and discuss training needs.

If you have done some programming at school or college you may have come across most of those ideas. You must accept, all the same, that real-world programming needs far more care than even an A level programming project. In commercial work a programmer may produce on average only a dozen lines of code a day. As major software suites consist of thousands of lines (or even more than a million) you can see why programming teams and project leaders are needed.

A level and higher qualifications are needed for success in programming. The personal skills needed are:

- ☐ the ability to think logically and clearly and express your thoughts and work neatly on paper;
- ☐ a sense of creativity;
- ☐ the ability to convert broad needs into an effective algorithm (to define a process as a clear sequence of steps, in other words);
- ☐ the ability to work steadily and with care and patience, and not let frustration get you down (seeking a neat solution to a problem or finding and dealing with a bug can be immensely frustrating until you succeed, and succeed you must);
- ☐ the ability to work a lot on your own, but also get on with other people, in particular close team members;
- ☐ an aptitude for figures;
- ☐ a good memory.

Programming can be tremendously exciting work. It can also be very tedious.

Specialist Organisations

There are three main types of firm here. The computer bureaux (which are becoming less common) have their own computer system and provide computing services to other firms that have none or not enough. Software houses are growing in importance (but many fail); their role is to develop and market software to meet the needs of specific clients or a particular field. Technical support services (also growing) provide repair and maintenance engineers and technicians.

The computer department of a large company is rather like a bureau in that each day its work varies greatly as it meets the needs of management and the firm's various departments. Even so, a computer department's tasks, other than general ones, will remain within a certain field: even a bureau that specialises in a single industry will find the work done to be much more varied. Some computer bureaux start life as computer departments that could not find enough work in-house; others come about when several fairly small companies agree to share the costs and the rewards of a single joint system.

Computer bureaux work in different ways. Thus customers can buy time as and when they need it or they may contract to have their work processed each week or month on a regular basis. The modern trend is IT based: each client has its own terminals and gains access to the computer bureau through a telephone line. The bureau's system processes the work and the results are sent back. We call this time sharing.

A new kind of service bureau is growing fast. It provides data-preparation services only for organisations without a data-preparation department and for those who can't cope with a sudden increase in work load. It is a fact of life in most companies involved with data preparation that the work load varies greatly over the year; data-preparation service bureaux exist to help smooth the demand and to save the problems of excessive overtime or short-time working. Some of these bureaux are also able to offer the more conventional services of a computer bureau as well.

All these operations need various types of people: computer operators, data controllers, terminal operators, programmers, systems analysts and O & M (organisation and method) officers. Who will employ you as what? Firms that use bureaux do not need programmers or systems analysts, or even computer operators, but they do need data controllers, terminal operators and

O & M officers and these people need to be very clear about what a computer can do. Such firms are also a good starting point for budding programmers and analysts. The most exciting prospect if you have such work in such a company is that you are likely to become deeply involved when your management decides to obtain their own computer system. Promotion can then be very rapid.

Service bureaux, on the other hand, will not use O & M officers, as some of them do not have terminal operators as they only process the work. However, they are good places to get work as an operator or data controller; bureaux employ a lot of them and are prepared to train people for these jobs. Programmers and systems analysts get the most variety in a computer bureau.

There are also software houses: organisations that sell the services and products of programmers, systems analysts and (sometimes) operators. A software house is an excellent starting point for trainee programmers as they have the opportunity to learn from a number of experienced colleagues, the variety of work is enormous and there is enough junior work to get you off the ground. Organisations that sell a similar service for O & M officers do not often take trainees as they do not have the call for people who have not been through an extensive O & M training course.

Most smaller software houses concentrate on only one field of activity. You may know those that publish home software, games or educational programs, but meeting the needs of business and industry is common too, and this is much more important and much more lucrative.

Computer bureaux normally have a number of clients to whom they provide their services through long-term contracts. Such arrangements are much rarer in the case of software houses: their work tends to come unpredictably in the form of individual commissions. This is a major reason for software houses to get into selling their products (and sometimes those produced elsewhere); it is also a major reason why such firms can go out of business as good cash flow is so hard to maintain.

Technical support firms can also have cash-flow problems if they do not build up a good bread-and-butter basis of long-term maintenance and breakdown contracts. They will also take the jam of repairs for other customers. However, they do not need to sell themselves as hard in this context as software houses, for their outlay on capital equipment is lower and their staff levels are more stable. There are many kinds of maintenance and breakdown contract in the industry. The best and dearest, but the most effective from the manager's point of view, are those which require an engineer to come on site within no more than a few hours of a fault's being reported. The annual cost of such a contract is typically at least 10 per cent of the purchase price of the installation. In return for that, the maintenance company must ensure that its staff are properly supplied with manuals, tools and spare parts and that they keep up to date by frequent attendance at special training courses.

The maintenance and repair systems that have started to appear to look after the cheap home, school and office microcomputers are much less costly. Here the owner is usually expected to deliver the machine to the repair shop when work is needed; there is no contract now, but simply payment for work done and parts used. However, as the IBM PC and its clones become common, more and more little companies are finding they can arrange regular maintenance contracts like those described above.

It is true that microelectronic systems are highly reliable; they do not often give trouble once they are run in. However, the mechanical parts associated with them (disc drives, printer heads and belts, cooling fans and so on) are a different matter; as in any other type of equipment, these give more and more trouble as they grow older. Specialist peripheral maintenance is needed therefore and this is a rapidly growing area as a result. If you think of going in for this kind of work, never forget that what the clients want is courteous, speedy and efficient service. It is worth your while therefore to make very sure that that is what you can provide them with. You will also need a vehicle and a clean driving licence.

One unusual aspect of the field of computer-system maintenance and repair is that it is possible to enter it from outside the industry. A number of people turn to such work after serving as broadcast technicians or working in the domestic video market or in related fields in the armed forces (such as telecommunications, navigation systems and radar). This is also an area where it is fairly easy to obtain grants for training.

Something has been said already about technical service work in Chapter 5. There too you will find other ideas for jobs on your own in the computer industry. However, there is a very new type of specialist organisation, that offering facilities management. Facilities management involves the outside firm taking all the responsibility for running a company's computer installation. An efficient and effective team is put on site and kept up to strength at all times; thus the parent company loses all the worry of recruitment for and management of the department. As a result it can get on with its own business in peace.

As this kind of service is provided under an annual contract, the facilities management company has a real incentive to provide an excellent service; because of this, it is claimed, the costs of running the computer department can be cut by as much as a quarter. A company's main worry, to set off against that saving of money, is whether the facilities management team can really understand what the client needs. If you enter this field therefore you must ensure that you can communicate well and obtain a precise statement of the work that the department is to undertake.

Two other areas of activity need to be mentioned here, though the numbers of firms involved in each case are far smaller than in those mentioned. First is the hiring (short-period rental) and leasing (long-period rental) of hardware; second is insurance.

As far as renting (short or long term) is concerned, many different schemes are on offer from firms specialising in the field. A surprisingly large number of these firms include financial services (loan arrangement); this adds significantly to the overheads of running their business, already high because of the capital costs of the equipment they must own and the maintenance services they must offer. Some of these companies specialise in second-hand hardware.

Most computer insurance is provided by the traditional insurance companies which have, to a greater or lesser extent, decided to move into this important and lucrative field. The law does not allow a person or group to set up as an insurance company without a great many conditions being met. The same applies to insurance broking (giving advice on insurance and arranging policies). The only simple way for a newcomer to get into the computer-insurance field is as an insurance consultant (often called a computer-risk specialist). Consultants may be concerned with all aspects of security and safety as well as with actual insurance. Some companies in this area offer stand-by hardware to clients in a fix, either ready to deliver or up and running at the end of a phone line.

Hardware Production

Apart from the usual support staff needed by any design and production company, the main need in this sector of the industry is for top-class engineers. Work of that nature is almost always closed except to graduates and for them the ladder to the top is a long one climbed fairly slowly. Certainly, in this field there is a great deal of mobility, with people moving up by moving from one firm to another. Of course, there is, and always will be, room for the clever-ideas person, but don't forget that old saying: genius is 1 per cent inspiration and the rest is perspiration.

Work in this field is divided into research and development (often handled in universities, the largest companies and the military) and design and production (mainly the province of free enterprise). Research tends to be into materials rather than devices; it is only when research produces results that the development people start working on uses. Design involves working toward actual devices and systems, turning the ideas into pilot products. The final stage is production of actual units for sale.

A range of support services is needed throughout, so there are plenty of openings for secretarial and information-handling staff, programmers, systems analysts, writers, technicians, librarians and sales people; these have been dealt with in earlier chapters, however.

CASE STUDY

Pat, a polytechnic honours graduate in electronic engineering, is part of a team working on the development of new hardware for a large computer importing company. The company has close links with the nearby university and one of Pat's roles is to assist with liaison in research and development. Much of the research is fairly short term, the attempt being to control microprocessors working simultaneously at high speed to produce effective parallel processing.

The field relates fairly closely to Pat's work experience on the sandwich course and to the mini-research project undertaken in the final year. However, there is now more money, more equipment, more chance to explore interesting new angles, more people with exciting ideas to think about. And more time too: while the project is urgent, Pat knows that it may take several years to get the circuits working properly and reliably and then perhaps several years more to design and produce working hardware based on the system they hope to develop.

Despite that seemingly lengthy timetable Pat feels under a lot of pressure to produce results, but enjoys the pressure and the challenge enough to be happy to work late in the laboratories and do a lot of reading at home. Are there thoughts of fame and fortune in Pat's mind? Maybe there are, but they are hidden. Certainly, Pat seems to enjoy the work greatly and to welcome each new problem that arises. Who can ask more from a job?

Conclusions

Programmers form the largest single group of people employed in the computer industry itself. Their work involves precise logical use of knowledge and skills; it involves much working alone as well as part of a team. People in the field have plenty of chance of promotion, but experience does not come quickly.

Computer bureaux, though in decline, will still need people for a number of years. Their work is very varied, so that if you join one you can gain a wide picture of the computer world quickly. Software houses are growing but do not all provide job security; all the same, they are a good opening for programmers and systems analysts. Technical-support firms are great for technicians and engineers with ambitions in electronics; they provide security and good prospects.

Salaries

Early 1987 salary ranges were:

Programming: £5000–£19,000
Technical support: £7000–£20,000
Technical support management: £15,000–£25,000

Chapter 7

Looking for Work

Standard and Specialist Sources of Help

The obvious places to look for work first are general and selective employment agencies and government employment offices, such as your local Jobcentre. Also, most areas have specialist agencies who deal in computer staff only. The advantage of going round these is that they can help you to decide on the type of computer work that would suit you best. There are far too many (hundreds to be more exact) of these computer employment agencies to list them all here, most being fairly small but expert in a very local geographical area. However, if you visit your local reference library you can consult *The Computer Users' Year Book* (published each year). This contains an extensive list of agencies and what they specialise in.

Here we simply give details of a few of the larger such companies around the country that have a good reputation at the time of writing and have a good number of consultants with experience in the computing and IT field. Look in your Yellow Pages directory for details of others; the headings to use are *Employment agencies and consultancies* and *Secretarial and office services*. Note, finally, that, as with address lists elsewhere in this book, only the headquarters' addresses are given; because the firms listed are among the largest, most will have many offices around the country so check the business phone book.

Brown & Snook
Wren House
Sutton Court Road
Sutton
Surrey SM1 4TL

BTT
Dean Clough Office Park
Halifax HX3 5AX

Computer Search
Drayton House
Gordon Street
London WC1H 0AM

Compuvac Personnel Services
121 City Road
London EC1V 1JB

Coopers & Lybrand
25 Farringdon Street
London EC4A 4AQ

Data Dimension
8 Portland Street
Southampton

Delta Personnel
8 Radnor Avenue
Harrow
Middlesex HA1 1SB

John Dalton Partnership
4 Post Office Avenue
Southport
Lancashire PR9 OUS

Eurolink Group
102 Queen's Road
Brighton BN1 3YF

Guardian Staff Services
St James's House
Salford
Lancashire M6 5JA

Hunterskil Knight
14 Old Park Lane
London W1Y 4NL

KPG Computer Support Services
Cobden House
Park Lane
Richmond
Surrey TW9 2RA

Lorien Computer Services
OCS House
Servia Road
Leeds LS7 1NJ

Management Personnel
2 Swallow Place
London W1R 7AA

MDA Computer Group
The Grove
Slough
Berkshire SL1 1RH

Recruitment Consultancy
31 Southampton Row
London WC1B 5HJ

Rendeck
8 Nelson Street
Southend
Essex SS1 1EF

Scott-Grant
26 Cross Street
Manchester M2 7AN

Specialist Computer
Recruitment
Equity & Law House
Great Charles Street
Birmingham B3 3JY

Stirling Computer Support Services
44 Richmond Road
Kingston
Surrey KT2 5EE

Thornton Baker Associates
Fairfax House
Fulwood Place
London WC1V 6DW

Top-class recruitment companies no longer just take in names of companies and potential employees and hope to match; they have effective techniques for personnel analysis. Thus they can assess the individual's abilities and the company's needs very precisely. Aptitude tests and interviews should be the norm for people looking to them for jobs, while much time with the employing company needs to be spent in finding out exactly what their wants may be. Personnel management and a good grasp of training opportunities should be offered by such an agency.

As in other areas of the office employment world, there are very many companies who specialise in providing computer personnel on a temporary basis. The list that follows gives only the largest of these: the ones that cover all or nearly all of mainland Britain and also keep people on their register at all levels from data-preparation staff to systems analysts. You can refer to the sources mentioned above for details of the many others.

Buick Computer Services
72 Rochester Row
London SW1P 1JU

Compucare Computer Systems
6 Oak Lane
Twickenham
Middlesex TW1 3PE

Compuvac Personnel Services
121 City Road
London EC1V 1JB

Data Processing People
26 Red Lion Square
London WC1R 4RL

Datapower Computer Contracts
21 Cork Street
London W1X 1HB

Effectia Gravis
66 Wardour Street
London W1V 3HP

KPG Computer Support Services
Cobden House
Park Lane
Richmond
Surrey TW9 2RA

Span Computer Contracts
43 Great Windmill Street
London W1V 7PA

TLP
Enterprise House
Homesdale Road
Bromley
Kent BR2 9TE

Trident Computer Services
38 Victoria Road
Farnborough
Hampshire GU14 7UD

The other place to look for work at anything but the lowest levels (where Jobcentres, local press and local agencies should be enough) is in the many specialist computer newspapers and magazines. Here you will find a huge variety of jobs advertised. In this way you will also pick up the names of recruitment agencies, as most of the better ones advertise in the various papers.

It is not likely that any of your local libraries will carry many of these periodicals; there is a large number of them, covering many hundred job vacancies at all levels each week. You may well be able to refer to these periodicals at your school, college or university computing-centre library, or find someone who can get them for you. Though many of them are free, it is not easy for non-graduates fresh from education or training to get on the mailing lists, and anyway that takes time.

The Computer Users' Year Book also has a comprehensive list of computer users and the equipment they use. You could write straight to some of these, especially if they are near where you live or are in an area where you would like to work. The other advantage of this is that you can address your letter direct to the data-processing manager as his or her name is usually given in the book (though, of course, such information goes out of date fairly fast).

However, be prepared for a long hard struggle along this particular road. Writing a lot of letters about yourself takes a lot of time and stationery and is not cheap. You will also find you don't get many replies. The best thing is to compose a short letter asking for any brochures about work in the company and how you can find out about vacancies. This letter should be clear and in good English (check all doubtful spellings). There is nothing wrong with handwritten letters here, but neatly typed or word-processed ones are good too. Use proper letter paper: certainly, do not write such important material on paper torn from a notebook or pad (many people do!). Also, avoid photocopying your letter even if it is typed or word processed: you mustn't make it look like junk mail, for the people you're writing to get enough of that already.

Other places to try include the computer companies themselves. Most of the larger ones run service bureaux and/or software houses of their own, and are also in constant touch with users' needs. The other advantage of talking to computer companies is that they will be able to advise you where to go to seek a particular type of position.

Naturally, if you decide first to take some sort of course, the institute you attend will assist you at the end.

Government Agencies

Don't forget to consult your local Jobcentre, employment office or careers office, as well as specialist careers staff at your school, college or university. They will be able to advise you on national vacancies as well as knowing about local firms and the training opportunities in your area.

For school-leavers the Manpower Services Commission Youth Training Scheme (YTS) is designed to give 16–18-year-olds basic training in such areas as new technology; this is often achieved through Information Technology Centres (ITeCs). ITeCs are usually based in offices or factory units and are run by local authorities and/or private sponsors. However, attendance at an ITeC or on any other YTS course does not often lead to any formal qualification, for the courses are mainly practical. All the same, it will give people considering a career in the computer industry some initial contact.

For older people the MSC's Restart, Job Training Scheme and TOPS courses are well worth finding out about. These, like the YTS scheme, are being developed all the time, so for current details contact your careers officer. If that is a problem, get in touch with your local Manpower Services Commission Vocational Education Training Group office. Look in the phone book or obtain the address from your nearest regional centre as listed below:

LONDON	01-836 1213
MIDLANDS	021-643 6338
NORTHERN	0632 326181
NORTH WEST	061-833 0251
SCOTLAND	031-225 8500
SOUTH EAST	0256 29266
SOUTH WEST	0272 273710

WALES	0222 388588
YORKSHIRE and HUMBERSIDE	0532 446299

For Graduates

The Central Services Unit (CSU) for university and polytechnic careers and appointments services has been created by the UK universities as a central point of information for students completing studies at degree level. Employers are encouraged to contact the unit with job-vacancy details and students using the unit can find out details of any of those vacancies. The unit serves people who are graduates, either those looking for their first appointment, or those seeking a change of work after two or three years of employment, as well as people who have not completed their higher-education courses successfully.

Two publications are available: *Current Vacancies* and *Forward Vacancies*. You can use these in conjunction with *ROGET*, the register of graduate employment and training. Further information regarding these services can be obtained from the director of the Central Services Unit (Crawford House, Precinct Centre, Oxford Road, Manchester M13 9EP; 061-273 4233).

It may also be worth talking to your local professional and executive register (PER) Officer; make contact through your local employment office. PER is very good at placing higher-level staff and have an excellent procedure for interviewing and aiding people looking for posts. Their weekly *Executive Post* details all the vacancies they know about and they have offices in 37 major centres in the country.

Finally, there are a number of institutions that are directly connected with computing; approach them for further information. Here's the list, but also refer to Chapter 11 for other sources of help.

Association of Professional
Computer Consultants
109 Baker Street
London W1M 2BH
01–267 7144

British Computer Society
13 Mansfield Street
London W1M 0BP
01-637 0471

Computer Services Industry
Training Council
5th floor
Hanover House
73/74 High Holborn
London WC1 6LE
01-242 5049

Institute of Data Processing
Management
18 Henrietta Street
London WC2E 8NU
01-240 3305

Institution of Analysts and
Programmers
39 Fourth Cross Road
Twickenham
Middlesex TW2 5EL
01-898 0195

Operational Research Society
14 Waterloo Street
Birmingham B2 5TX
021–643 0236

UK Information Technology
Organisation
10th floor
Millbank Tower
London SW1P 4QS
0420 58534

The next organisation is the professional body to approach for information on O & M:

Institute of Management Services
1 Cecil Court
London Road
Enfield
Middlesex EN2 6DD
01–363 7452

Chapter 8

Getting a Job

Your Application

The last chapter showed that looking for jobs is a two-pronged attack. On the one hand, you visit Jobcentres and agencies and scan the press for adverts for particular jobs. On the other, you make brief general approaches to companies of interest. Only in the last case are you likely not to need to apply for work formally. It is possible that an open approach to a given company may lead to your being invited for an interview, perhaps after filling in a personal-details form. The same is the usual practice of agencies. There are up to three components to an application for a job. It is often the case that on writing for details of a given job, graduates will be asked to complete a form, supply a curriculum vitae (c.v.) and send the two in with a covering letter (usually, non-graduates can dispense with the c.v.).

Whatever the nature of the application, it has one single function. The firm uses it to decide which few of the dozens or hundreds of applicants it would like to interview. If the application gives a poor impression, or sounds as if the person concerned is not very special, that is the end of it – therefore view it as a ticket to an interview.

An application form normally asks about your personal, educational and career details and your interests; it will carry spaces for other relevant information and the names and addresses of your referees. Referees are the people who have agreed to say something in your support. You may use your teacher and/or previous and current employers, including those for holiday work if you are just leaving education or training. Choose your referees with care (they should know you well and recently and have some knowledge of how well you work) and you must ask their permission before giving their names to a prospective employer. This last point does not apply if you want to give your current employer as a referee but wish to keep secret the fact that you are looking elsewhere. In that case give the name with a note to say that he or she should not be approached yet. Draft your answer before tackling the printed form and then complete it in black ball-point pen; do so very neatly and clearly and do not leave any questions without an answer (even if you answer a question in your letter instead, you should say so). Note that you can complete the form with a typewriter or word processor instead of by hand, but this is very fiddly and best avoided. If you are doing a lot of forms, choose two or three of the most detailed and have copies made after you have filled them in. Keep these copies for they will be useful to refer to now and later. Such reference material helps as you fill in other forms, but is of particular value if you are asked to send a c.v. As the story of your life it therefore should give the same information as a form: details of yourself, your education, training, experience and interests. Usually, if a firm sends you a form as well as asking for a c.v. the form will be a very brief one. The major difference between the contents of a form and of a c.v. is that a certain amount of comment is allowed in the latter. Thus you can say why certain qualifications and/or experience are relevant to the job concerned and highlight the relevance of such things as your post-experience training programme. Your c.v. can be typed or (even better) word processed. However, because it can contain specific comments, having a number of photocopies made for general use may not be wise. Word processing is the best method, for that allows changes to meet the needs of a given case easily.

Now we'll briefly run through what you should put in your c.v. You'll have to supply your own details, of course, but that's why you'll do well to keep copies of a couple of fully completed application forms. Start with who you are, giving both family name and all given names, your correspondence address (and home address if that is not the same) and your contact telephone number(s). Make it as easy as possible for the prospective employer to get in touch with you; never include complicated instructions about where messages can be left for you. If your phone is usable only between certain hours then show this on the form. The easier it is for the employer to contact you, the greater your chance of an interview.

Next outline your formal education. This will be the most important section if you have just left school or college. List secondary schools and any colleges or universities attended, with dates, exam results, diplomas and degrees. If you haven't worked before it's a good idea to include all subjects taken and grades. List what sports you participated in and what teams, societies or clubs you belonged to at school (especially those such as chess, computing and debating). In all these activities indicate if you held any position of responsibility, such as rugby captain, debating-society secretary or school chess champion. Don't be modest: remember you are selling yourself. Employers place great emphasis on school activities and positions held. Many believe that to have been, for instance, sports champion or club officer shows signs of leadership, and this will be an asset to your working career. If you have been a prefect or won any scholastic medals or special awards, mention these too. Don't be modest, but don't ramble on either!

Follow the details of your education and qualifications with notes on any relevant training you have had. (Of course, almost any training is relevant.) One or two years in the YTS (give details of placements as well), a fortnight's work experience, training courses followed in your past and present jobs if any – all these should go on. If you have already started work, it is good to show that you've made an effort to receive training, especially if this is voluntary.

Now comes your employment experience. Starting with your present or most recent job, and working backwards, give the name of each firm, your title and position held and your major responsibilities. Also give the name of your immediate superior(s) to make it easy for the prospective employer to find out more. If, however, you don't want anyone at your present firm to know you're looking elsewhere, make a note like this: 'Please do not approach at this stage'. As with referees, this is quite normal practice, so you need not feel shy about it. Show the start and finish dates for each job and give the dates of any promotions. Don't leave gaps by the way: if you were out of work for a while or took a break for family reasons, say so. Keep your text brief. Don't exaggerate and don't list all your achievements if there are lots of them: leave something for the interview. Remember you want to whet the reader's appetite to know more about you. You should also state why you left each job, the normal reason being, of course, because you had better prospects at the next stop. It's good to bear in mind, by the way, that changing jobs too often is a bad sign to the readers: they may think you are a trouble-maker, unable to settle down, or a bad risk in some other way. Reasons for leaving such as 'disagreement with management' or 'could not get on with immediate senior' can be damning on a c.v., so try to find some other reason. Wait until the interview to tell the facts, and then tell them truthfully: someone may have checked. At least at the interview you can defend yourself and explain your reasons fully.

If you are a school-leaver or a fresh graduate and have held some vacation jobs, or if you work in the evenings or weekends, show this too in the section of the c.v. Indicate what you did and for how long.

The last part should list hobbies and outside interests. Here too, say so if you have been an officer in any of the organisations you have belonged to. Give a prospective employer something to talk to you about; hobbies and interests are a good thing to start off with. By getting into a spontaneous conversation you and the interviewer will be able to talk more easily and get to know each other better.

It has been suggested already that you type or word process your c.v. and it goes without saying that you should make it neat, clear and beautifully laid out. Another suggestion in this context is to place the c.v. in a plastic envelope or even bind it in a folder. A bit extravagent you may think, but consider the effect on the employer of finding a well-bound file among a hundred applications of paper pages. The chances of the file being picked up first or put on top of the pile are very good. It also shows that a little trouble has been taken and that you have thought hard about your application. Remember again that you are selling yourself for what may (now or later) be a very well-paid job.

The final component of your application is the letter that covers the rest. At the very least you should say (in a fairly friendly, but polite and concise way) what the job is you are writing for and why you want it. The last bit means saying something about the opportunities you feel the job can provide and how you feel your background is particularly useful to the firm. This letter does not need to be lengthy (even for high-level jobs a page or two is enough), but you should know that it is possible that the letter may be all the reader has time to check. In other words if the letter is poor, the rest of your work may go straight into the bin. People differ as to whether application letters should be written or typed (or word processed). The longer the letter and the higher the qualifications needed for the job, the less useful is writing it. However, there are still people around who reckon handwriting tells them a lot about the writer, though neatness, good English and correct spelling are essential in any case. Read the advert and/or job details with care: maybe you will be told that you should write by hand.

Reading advert and job details with care is a good idea anyway! Not only should they say clearly what sort of person the firm is looking for, but they should say things like closing date, job reference number and to whom exactly you should apply. If you get any of those wrong, you are likely to waste your application. There is nothing wrong, by the way, in phoning the firm to ask for further details, as long as your questions are sensible ones and not just an obvious publicity ploy. Indeed, for higher-level jobs asking to make an initial visit to look round is quite in order.

This leads on to an important piece of advice. The more you can find out about a potential employer the better. You should be aware of the type of work they do and how they do it; you should have some idea of their importance in the community; you would benefit even by finding out the personal hobby-horses and prejudices of the people who might interview you. This is not just on the grounds of 'forewarned is forearmed' (though that is a useful little motto): it is also very effective if you can impress possible employers with your understanding of their work and their importance. Carry out this research by talking to people. If you can find one or two acquaintances who work for the company, all the better, but just chatting to staff and customers in the local shops or library will give you useful hard information. A large company will feature in business directories, held in the reference section of main public libraries. To repeat the advice given in Chapter 2, if you understand something of the technical language of the work in question, you will again get valuable points.

The Interview

The interview is the next stage in getting a job. Once you have been asked to go for an interview, it will give a good impression if you confirm the date and time by phone or (better) by typed letter. Also remember to note date, time and place in your diary so you don't forget to go. Of course, if you are offered an interview for a time when you have one already, don't be afraid to say so. Many people try to juggle their times because they think that if they turn an interview down they will lose the job, but this is unlikely.

The interview itself is very important: you are selling yourself as a package. At interview, when the package is unwrapped, make sure the goods look acceptable. First impressions should not count for a lot, but they do, and are therefore crucial. The first thing the interviewer sees is you and the way you dress. The clothes themselves are not too significant. What is important is the impression you create when you are first seen. It is far better therefore to be conservative and safe and not to give your interviewer any cause for prejudice.

Here are some points that employers tend to like, even if only subconsciously.

- ☐ Ensure that your clothes are clean and nicely pressed.
- ☐ Have your hair well kept, properly combed, not too long (men) and tied back (women with long hair).
- ☐ Wear shirt and tie (men).
- ☐ Wear a skirt rather than trousers (women).
- ☐ Wear clean shoes in a good state of repair.
- ☐ Don't arrive in the interview room loaded with carrier bags and coats and such (leave your outer coat with the secretary).

The next important matter is reaching the place of interview. Never be late. Nothing annoys employers more than applicants who arrive late for interviews. There are few good reasons for coming late (other than a strike or a snowstorm), and even then a phone call saying you're delayed, and why, will make an enormous difference. If an applicant can't be bothered to be on time for an interview for a job, how reliable will he or she be in the daily routine, if employed? Best aim to arrive 15 or 20 minutes in advance of the stated time: that'll allow for some delay and also give you a chance to relax when you get there.

Ensure your promptness by:

- ☐ finding out the exact location of your interview;
- ☐ knowing precisely what public transport or route will get you there;
- ☐ establishing exactly how far the bus or train stops from your destination, so you know in advance how far you'll have to walk;
- ☐ finding out what the parking facilities are like and where they are if you intend using your own transport;
- ☐ doing a dry run beforehand (at the right time of day) so you know exactly how long it takes you to get there.

If you find that after all you are going to be late, phone as soon as you can to let your interviewer know. If you arrive early you have time to catch your breath and collect your thoughts, so you have a better chance of being relaxed at the interview. It may also give you an opportunity to look around and perhaps study a relevant brochure or two.

Go to your interview with a folder of your testimonials, school or other reports and certificates, the job details, a copy of your application and the letter stating the appointment. If you have any relevant samples of your work put these in too. Make sure your folder is neat so you can lay your hands on any document quickly.

When you arrive for an interview you may be asked to fill in a form. Have your own pen ready and do not rush this. Use your copy of your application to ensure that the information you record is exactly the same as you sent in before. Fill the form in as neatly as you can, after reading each question very carefully. (Reading before writing will cut down many errors and crossings out.) Don't leave any parts out. You may also be asked to sit an aptitude test before or after the interview. If this is the case you will probably be warned in advance. See the next section for some advice on this.

In the interview itself, you will be asked certain standard questions for which you should have your answers prepared well in advance. It is important that you show a degree of confidence at the interview and if you can be prepared for such questions, with reasonable answers not given in parrot fashion but in a businesslike manner, you will impress. Typical questions you will be asked concern:

- ☐ your hobbies or interests;
- ☐ favourite subjects of study;
- ☐ why you wish to work with computers;
- ☐ why you want to work with this particular firm;
- ☐ your family background;
- ☐ the aspects of computer usage that interest you most;
- ☐ why the firm should hire you.

You may well consider taking your preparation a stage further; it is possible to analyse each job and compile a list of those qualities necessary to perform that job well. Usually, about a dozen qualities will sum up a job pretty accurately. As as example, those suggested for a programmer are as follows.

- ☐ technical knowledge/proficiency;
- ☐ ability to learn;
- ☐ job motivation;
- ☐ attention to detail
- ☐ initiative;
- ☐ creativity;
- ☐ problem-solving ability;
- ☐ working with others;
- ☐ tenacity and patience;
- ☐ communication skills;
- ☐ self-discipline.

(You should research the job you are applying for by reference to other parts of this book and prepare your list of qualities. Quite comprehensive job descriptions will also be found in the *Computer Users' Year Book*.) Having done this, think of examples of your past performance which illustrate your proficiency in the qualities listed. This will equip you to answer questions you are asked and to provide practical examples of your effectiveness in these areas.

An interview is often in two parts. The first involves the interviewer(s) asking you questions and in the second you have a chance to ask them things.The interview itself is not an inquisition, though it may feel so, especially if you are interviewed by more than one person. Be prepared for that, but don't let it worry you. If you have several interviewers at once, always reply to the person who asks a given question, but look round at all the interviewers when talking.

The first part of the interview will be judged in two ways: first, what your answers are and, second, how you get these answers across. You must speak good plain English. Do not mutter, put on an affected accent, or use words that you're not used to. Try to make the interviewer feel at home; answer each question fully, rather than with a simple 'yes' or 'no'. On the other hand, don't ramble on: try to be brief and concise without being abrupt. Don't be diverted in your answers and then wander off the subject: stick to the point. When talking of computers or the industry, or your interests, show some enthusiasm; emotion and enthusiasm usually influence an interviewer, even a very dry or dull one.

The second part of the interview gives you a chance to ask the questions. You may like to find out about:

- ☐ the size of the department and of the team you would be working with if you get the job;
- ☐ who you would report to (don't be shy to ask to see an organisation chart);
- ☐ the nature and likely speed of promotion;
- ☐ leave periods and hours of work;
- ☐ special perks (canteen, discounts, transport assistance and so on);
- ☐ how long training lasts and the existence of further training courses.

It's very important that you don't just ask about benefits (money, perks, holidays) at this stage. If you do, that will give the impression that you aren't interested in the job itself but only in what you can get out of it. Even if that is the case, don't give this impression! Indeed, if the advert and interviewer don't mention salary and other benefits, it's best to ask about these only if and when you are offered the job. In that way you get into a far stronger negotiating position. If you haven't seen the place where you would work if appointed, ask about that too.

Some people wonder if they can smoke during an interview. Don't! Even if you are offered a cigarette and are feeling desperate because of the strain, don't accept. (If you are a heavy smoker who can't get by without a drag for several hours on end, you ought to know that smoking is banned in many offices and computer areas nowadays.)

Now for some smaller points.

- ☐ Don't finish your interviewer's sentences, for this means you aren't listening. Never interrupt. Don't swear, however bad the language the interviewer uses. Lastly, smile and look pleasant (no one likes to see a glum face).
- ☐ If you are shown around, try to look carefully at the attitudes of the people you come across and if possible speak to them. Remember these are the folk you could be working with.
- ☐ At the end of the interview do not leave until you've been told how and when you will be informed if you are successful. If you are offered the job then and there, ask the interviewer if you can ring back the next day as you wish to think about it first.
- ☐ After the interiew think about all you've been told; decide too if that is where you wish to work and whether those are the people with whom you'd like to spend your days. If you are offered the job at least you'll know whether you want it or not. And if you don't fancy the place, accept only if you are truly desperate; misery at work is best avoided, and don't forget it looks bad if you leave a post too quickly.

Aptitude Tests

Many firms (but not yet all) will ask you to do an aptitude test before or after your interview, so you should be prepared for this. The questions depend on job level, but the general nature of the tests used is described below; it may well be worthwhile to get up some speed in answering such questions.

For school and college leavers, the tests are normally on numeracy (arithmetic exercises, juggling numbers), English (spelling, juggling letters – it helps to write down the alphabet on a scrap of paper before you start); 2D and 3D figures (comparison of like and opposite of similar and dissimilar figures); IQ (all sorts of funny questions). To help you prepare, first, borrow or buy books of tests like these and get some practice doing them. The Penguin books *Know your own IQ* and *Check your own IQ* by Professor H J Eysenck are particularly useful as far as so-called intelligence testing is concerned. Second, ensure you remember the simple rules of multiplication, division, fractions and percentages: all the things you learned in mental arithmetic. Thirdly, when you are given a test, read it very carefully. If it is explained to you, don't be so nervous or in such a hurry to start that you are afraid to ask questions if there is something you don't understand. Ask questions before the test starts. You may not be allowed to ask afterwards: most tests are timed.

If you are a graduate and/or are applying for a senior position you may instead be asked to undergo extensive psychological tests. On the other hand, if you are going for a job as a keyboard or computer operator, the firm may give you a practical test. In either case keep cool and you won't go far wrong.

You won't lose a job you have already because you fail a test. Tests are designed mainly to see if you have an aptitude before you start. If you score below a certain percentage range you will be told so and possibly not get any further. On the other hand, if you have applied for a job as a programmer you may be considered for data control if the test shows you have more aptitude for that type of work.

In general, aptitude tests are good things: they mean that applicants are not going into jobs for which they are unsuited. It is important to remember if you fail that you have failed only that particular test. It does not mean that you aren't qualified for anything else.

Part 2

Chapter 9

Training and Personal Development

Training Courses

The possible need for initial and in-service training has been mentioned several times in this book. For low-level jobs the training gained at school or at college, or with the Youth Training Scheme (YTS), is enough to get you started. Higher up and later the education and training you have had, while still important, becomes second to your actual experience.

When you find work, you will also find that your organisation provides enough training to start you off, to keep you going and (if you are more lucky) to help you progress up the ladder. You should not find it too hard to join other in-house courses in fields close to, but different from, your actual work. Doing that will rarely cost you more than spare time and will put good marks on to your record as well as helping you be better prepared for promotion and/or future applications.

For one reason or another, however, you may decide to go for further training without having a job, in particular because you feel this will ease your getting work later. Grants may be available. As well as government training schemes (see following and Chapter 11) and what Open College and Open University offer, you'll find many companies that put on training courses for people outside. Also, manufacturers usually have training divisions and may offer courses to outside students. Such companies are listed at the end of the chapter; contact them for details.

A number of the many firms which run computer courses are now listed. There is a great diversity in these courses and training is available for most types or work. Some firms will train you and, if you come up to standard, offer you a job. Others will train you and then attempt to place you in a job elsewhere. Try to avoid the ones that don't offer either kind of incentive. Most courses are quite expensive, ranging from £50 for a few afternoons or evenings to several hundred pounds for a full programming package.

An important word of warning! You may have seen computer training advertised by commercial computer schools in the press, quoting very attractive salaries after course completion. Be wary: the salary quoted may be what can be expected after some years or may not be substantiated at all. Not all commercial computer schools are suspect, but some are, so it is well to be absolutely sure what is on offer before you enrol. Areas you should explore include the following.

- ☐ What percentage of applicants are accepted as suitable for training? If the value is very high, be more wary.
- ☐ Will they tell you after training if you are not suitable and also refund your fees? If not, be more wary.
- ☐ Will they accept part of their fee from your future earnings? If not, be more wary.
- ☐ Is there a placement service at the end of the course? If not ....
- ☐ Are they under contract to train personnel for other industrial employers or government? If not ....
- ☐ Do the premises and equipment look adequate, clean and well run?

The National Computing Centre (NCC) has a code of practice which certain commercial computer schools agree to follow; while this is not a guide to the quality of training, the subscribing schools accept certain obligations regarding what they offer to their clients. At the time of writing the NCC also supervises a highly regarded Threshold Scheme in data processing for school-leavers; it is possible that this may become part of YTS, but it could be worth checking if the course is offered in your area.

The following training firms subscribe to the NCC code:

Allan D'Morias and Associates Ltd
60 High Street
Harrow
Middlesex HA1 3LL

Compucentres
1st floor
Drayton House
Gordon Street
London WC1H OAX

Computer Programming School
1 Golders Manor Drive
London NW11 9HU

Control Data Institute
77–79 Wells Street
London W1P 3RE

James Ross Associates
Suite 716
Crest Hotel
The Ringway
Preston PR1 1AU

School of Computer Technology
104–108 Oxford Street
London W1N 9FA

Triad Computer Services Ltd
21–23 City Buildings
Old Hall Street
Liverpool L3 9BT

Z Z Fisher
43 Bethune Road
London N16 5EE

In addition to the above companies which specially subscribe to the NCC code of conduct, there are others that concentrate on keyboard operator and/or word-processor-operator training. This does not fall within the NCC scheme, but you'll be particularly interested in such courses if you wish to enter data processing at this level. As with other such address lists in this book, the headquarters of each training firm only is given; many have training facilities elsewhere.

ADM
5 Headstone Road
Harrow
Middlesex HA1 1PL
01-863 0621

Alan Pearman Ltd
96 Chester Road
Huntington
Chester CH3 6BT
0244 46024

ASI UK
27a Carlton Drive
London SW15 2TE
01-788 8834

Centre Point
25 Oxford Street
London W1B 1RF
01-734 1052

Circuit UK
26 New Street
St Neots
Cambridgeshire PE19 1AJ
0480 217425

Commercial and Computer Services
Globe House
New Street
Chelmsford CM1 5GN
0245 350621

Compower
Walsall Road
Cannock
Staffordshire WS11 3HZ
05435 2511

Compucentre (London) Ltd
24 Stephenson Way
London NW1 2HD
01-388 0691

Computer Learning Centre
41 Charles Street
London W1X 7PB
01-493 8899

Computer Training Services
28 Churchill Way
Cardiff CF1 4DY

Computer Technology
Eaton Road
Hemel Hempstead
Hertfordshire HP2 7LB
0442 3272

Computing Services
Bow Street
Hanley
Staffordshire ST1 2LA
0782 286015

Datasolve Education
14 Old Park Lane
London W1Y 3LH
01-499 7099

Deltak
Skytech Centre
Poyle Road
Colnbrook
Slough SL3 0DS
0753 684588

Digitus
10 Bedford Street
London WC2E 9HE
01-379 6968

DTW Education Services
27 Clarence Square
Brighton BN1 2ED
0273 203636

Edutext
College House
Wright's Lane
London W8 5SH
01-937 9633

Haven Computer Services
8 Guilford Street
London WC1N 8DT
01-404 5603

Interface Network
17 Bilton Road
Basingstoke
Hampshire RG24 0LJ
0256 461191

Keyboard Training Ltd
Parkway House
Sheen Lane
London SW14 8LS
01-876 8661

Key Punch Agency
149 Balham Hill
London SW12 9DU
01-675 5454

Key Skill
Bognor Road
Rowhook
West Sussex RH12 3PS
0403 790218

Micromark
Adam Court
Bell Street
Henley
Oxfordshire RG9 2DM
04915 77926

MSS Services
31a Chapel Road
Worthing
Sussex BN11 1EG
0903 34755

NCR
2096 Coventry Road
Birmingham B26 3YU
021-742 2311

Pitman Computer Training
128 Long Acre
London WC2E 9AN
01-379 7517

Plusmark Business Systems
54 Moorbridge Road
Maidenhead
Berkshire SL6 8BN
0625 74661

Reach-a-Teacha
2 Hastings Court
Collingham
Wetherby
Yorkshire LS22 0DT
0937 72698

Sight and Sound Education
118 Charing Cross Road
London WC2H 0JR
01-379 3455

Teaching Aids
Denestead House
Station Road
New Milton
Hampshire BH25 6LD
0425 612911

Working in the Industry

Working with actual computer companies rather than with users has a number of advantages. Often the jobs are aimed at fresh graduates, but if you haven't a degree it is still not very hard to enter and work up (see also Chapter 6).

Companies that manufacture (or import) and sell computers require a lot of computer staff. The jobs described in previous chapters (systems analysts, programmers, operators and so on) are available in these organisations, although with them you will be likely to be one of many, and not quite such a specialist as in a private firm. For this reason you may find that salaries are often lower. However, to compensate for this, you will be at the forefront of computer development and your opportunities for career progression will be greater.

The software systems programmer will usually be a graduate with a degree in a subject like mathematics or computer science; he or she will look after a team of programmers and also these will probably be graduates. There will be a number of programmers (who may be non-graduates) too, used to give support to the customers just in the software house.

Work in computer companies also involves such jobs as research and development in both hardware and software. These are usually reserved for graduates who have specialised in computer science, mathematics and physics.

Training is another major area where many graduates are employed. The industry has poached a lot of school and college teachers for this purpose, especially in the fields of mathematics and science. Training is needed not only for the firm's own staff, but also for those of customers, and for this reason people with such subjects as accounting or business studies are also of likely value.

To work on the engineering aspects of manufacture and maintenance, you need to be a graduate in some kind of engineering, with an emphasis on electronics. This also applies to training in these fields; maintenance staff are being trained constantly as they join the company and as new equipment becomes available or is installed in any one engineer's territory.

Sales

Computer companies also need sales staff. You should not only know about the hardware and software you are selling, but also build up specialised knowledge of a specific aspect of commerce or industry (such as accounting, engineering and business studies). Top sales staff are usually graduates, especially in the larger companies. Selling computer hardware is not a job that requires foot-in-the-door tactics and quick-fire patter.

The sales side of the computer industry is an area where you can earn a lot of money (£12,000–£30,000) as most companies pay their sales staff commission as well as a basic salary. The commission is often worked out on the basis of sales above a certain level that is fixed each year for each person. The sales people in these companies are usually the elite because of the good money they earn and the business they bring in to the firm. Annual earnings as high as £250,000 are not unknown, but to get into that bracket requires exceptional talent and an outstanding knowledge of the industry. The average value is probably in the £30,000–£50,000 range.

Although some sales people enter this industry from other high-technology fields (such as modern office equipment or electronics), it is normal for one to progress through the ranks, so to speak. After some years in computing itself (hardware or software, development or applications), you would move into sales at a fairly low level, and work up as your experience and knowledge grow. The knowledge is essential; computer sales staff of the kind we are talking about here are involved with total systems rather than with hardware alone. Software and communications networks must also be tailored to the client's exact and likely future needs.

A new field of selling has opened up with the arrival of the microcomputer. Most micro manufacturers and importers do not market their own products; rather they rely on a dealer network (this is true also of major mainframe manufacturers as far as their micros are concerned). It follows therefore that many job opportunities are appearing both with these dealers and with the high-street retailers. The employers here are usually far less rigid about qualifications; as long as you are prepared to work hard, you'll find lack of formal qualifications no handicap.

Another field open to a young person who is not a good analyst or programmer, and who does not have a degree, is sales support. Many computer companies employ support staff who come in with the sales people and assist the user in preparing the organisation for the installation of a new computer system. They help to plan the layout of the computer areas, design forms, train staff and generally ease the traumatic experience of getting a new system of working under way. This is a very interesting field to be in; jobs are usually taken by people with three or four years' clerical experience who are then trained by the computer company. Sales support can lead to sales itself or, of course, to O & M (organisation and methods) and systems analysis.

Field Work

The field staff are the people who help the customers to maintain their systems in good working order. If you'd prefer to work in one office or factory, this work would not suit you: it involves moving from customer to customer as they ring in for engineering assistance and you could be on call at night too. In most companies there are various levels of field staff: specialists in certain equipment; general engineers able to repair all equipment; juniors who specialise in single items such as certain input and output devices. The qualification required for the full field engineer is usually a degree in electronic engineering but there are plenty of openings for others. Having worked for a while in an electronics company is also a very good recommendation. Most of the real training will be given by the company on their own equipment.

Britain's Main Computer Firms

This list is far from complete if you were to take it as showing all British computer manufacturers at the start of 1987. However, it includes all the big ones and most of the more important smaller ones. Note that the address and phone number given are for each company's headquarters. Often a firm will trade at a number of different places and have its factories in other parts of the country (or even overseas). However, at the addresses given you will be able to find out further details and speak to someone in the personnel department.

Acorn Computers
Fulbourn Road
Cambridge CB1 4JN
0223 245200

Altos Computer Systems
Manhattan House
High Street
Crowthorne
Berkshire RG11 7AT
0344 777911

Amstrad Electronics
169 King's Road
Brentwood
Essex CM14 4EF
0277 228888

Apple Computer (UK)
Eastman Way
Hemel Hempstead
Hertfordshire HP2 7HQ
0442 60244

Apricot Computers
Birmingham B15 3TR
021-454 9091

British Micro
Penfold Works
Imperial Way
Watford
Hertfordshire WD2 4YY
0923 48222

British Olivetti
86 Upper Richmond Road
London SW15 2UR
01-785 6666

Bromcom
417 Bromley Road
Bromley
Kent BR1 4PJ
01-697 8933

Burroughs Machines
Heathrow House
Cranford
Middlesex TW5 9QL
01-750 1400

Business Computer Systems
Sunrise Parkway
Milton Keynes MK14 6LJ
0908 665522

Canon UK
Manor Road
Wallington
Surrey SM6 0AJ
01-773 2156

CASU
Arundel Road
Uxbridge
Middlesex UB8 2RR
01-561 6820

Centre File
75 Leman Street
London E1 8EX
01-480 3000

Comcen Technology
45 Wychtree Street
Swansea SA6 8EX
0792 796000

Commodore Business Machines
1 Hunter's Road
Corby
Northamptonshire NN17 1QX
0536 205555

Computer Automation
Hertford House
Denham Way
Rickmansworth
Hertfordshire WD3 2XB
0923 771211

Computer Broking
68 Fulham Palace Road
London W6 9PL
01-741 8561

Control Data
179 Shaftsbury Avenue
London WC2H 8AR
01-240 3400

Dacoll
Gardners Lane
Bathgate
West Lothian EH48 1TP
0506 56565

Darkcrest
70 Newcomen Street
London SE1 1YT
01-403 5060

Data Controls
8 Longlands
Middlesbrough
Cleveland TS4 2JR
0642 241661

Data General
724 London Road
Hounslow
Middlesex TW3 1PD
01-572 7455

Dectrade
20 Ludlow Hill Road
Nottingham NG2 6HF
0602 235141

Digico Computers
58 Wilbury Way
Hitchin
Hertfordshire SE4 0TP
0462 37474

Digital Equipment
Imperial Way
Reading
Berkshire RG2 0TR
0734 868711

Ego Computer Systems
Stirling Way
Borehamwood
Hertfordshire WD6 2BT
01-207 4433

Electronic Data Processing
1 Tapton Park Road
Sheffield S10 3FG
0742 307373

Epson UK
388 High Road
Wembley
Middlesex HA9 6UH
01-902 8892

Ericsson Information Systems
1508 Coventry Road
Birmingham B25 8BN
021-707 3050

Europel Systems
Craven Road
Newbury
Berkshire RG14 5NE
0635 31074

Floating Point Systems
Apex House
London Road
Bracknell
Berkshire RG12 2TE
0344 56921

Fujitsu Europe
54 Jermyn Street
London SW1Y 6NQ
01-408 0043

Gemini Microcomputers
18 Woodside Road
Amersham
Buckinghamshire HP7 0BH
02403 28321

General Automation
Gerrards Cross
Buckinghamshire SL9 8EW
0753 889112

Gould Electronics
Grove Road
Sutton
Surrey SM1 1BY
01-643 8020

Harris Systems
Eskdale Road
Wokingham
Berkshire RG11 5TR
0734 698787

Hewlett Packard
Nine Mile Ride
Wokingham
Berkshire RG11 3LL
0344 773100

Honeywell Information Systems
Great West Road
Brentford
Middlesex TW8 9DH
01-568 9191

Husky Computers
345 Coleshill Road
Coventry CV6 5RW
0203 668181

IBM
PO Box 41
Portsmouth PO6 3AU
0705 321212

ICL International Computers
Bridge House
London SW6 3JX
01-788 7272

Imtec Computers
170 Honeypot Lane
Stanmore
Middlesex HA7 1LB
01-204 3456

Integrated Micro Products
Medomsley Road
Consett
Durham DH8 6SY
0207 503481

Jarogate
197 Lyham Road
London SW2 5PY
01-671 6321

John Elmer Office Equipment
Victoria Road
Burgess Hill
West Sussex RH15 9LR
04446 47771

Kalamazoo
Mill Lane
Northfield
Birmingham B31 2RW
021-475 2191

Kienzle Data Systems
224 Bath Road
Slough SL1 4DS
0753 33355

Logica UK
64 Newman Street
London W1A 4SE
01-637 9111

Lynx Business Machines
12 Deer Park Road
London SW19 3RJ
01-543 6611

MDB Systems
Unit 13 Wade Road
Basingstoke
Hampshire RG24 0NE
0256 464767

Modcomp
Molly Millar's Lane
Wokingham
Berkshire RG11 2JQ
0734 786808

Molecular Computers
Meadfield Road
Slough SL3 8AL
0753 44113

NBI
632 London Road
Isleworth
Middlesex TW7 4EZ
01-568 4242

Nokia
214 Kenton Road
Harrow
Middlesex HA3 8BT
01-907 2299

Norsk Data
Bath Road
Newbury
Berkshire RG13 1NU
0635 35544

North Star Computers
Enterprise House
Maxted Road
Hemel Hempstead
Hertfordshire HP2 7DX
0442 41266

Panasonic Industrial UK
280 Bath Road
Slough SL1 6JG
0753 73181

Philips Business Systems
Electra House
Colchester
Essex CO4 5BE
0206 575115

Plessey Microsystems
Water Lane
Towcester
Northamptonshire NN12 7JN
0327 50312

Prime Computers
2 Lampton Road
Hounslow
Middlesex TW3 1JW
01-572 7400

Pyramid Technology
St James' House
Knoll Road
Camberley
Surrey GU15 3SY
0276 63474

Rair
6 Upper St Martin's Lane
London WC2H 9EQ
01-836 6921

Research Machines
Mill Street
Oxford OX2 0BW
0865 249866

Sarel
Cosgrove Way
Luton
Bedfordshire LU1 1XL
0582 20121

Sharp Electronics
Thorp Road
Manchester M10 9BE
061-205 2333

Sinclair Research
25 Willis Road
Cambridge CB1 2AQ
0223 353204

Sony UK
South Street
Staines
Middlesex TW18 4PF
0784 61688

Sperry Computer Systems
Stonebridge Park
London NW10 8LS
01-965 0511

Stratus Computers
20 Cannon Street
London EC4M 6XD
01-248 8383

Systime Computers
Millshaw Science Park
Leeds LS11 0LT
0532 702277

Tensor Computers
Duke Street
Bedford MK43 3HR
0234 328688

Texas Instruments
Manton Lane
Bedford MK41 7PA
0234 67466

Torch Computers
Abberley House
Great Shelford
Cambridge CB2 5LQ
0223 841000

Triumph Adler
27 Goswell Road
London EC1M 7AJ
01-250 1717

Victor Technologies
Valley Centre
Gordon Road
High Wycombe
Buckinghamshire HP13 6EQ
0494 450661

Wang
661 London Road
Isleworth
Middlesex TW7 3EH
01-560 4151

Wicat Systems
403 London Road
Camberley
Surrey GU15 3HL
0276 686186

Zenith Data Systems
St John's Court
High Wycombe
Buckinghamshire HP11 1JX
0494 448781

Zeta Systems
Southgate
Bristol BS1 2NT
0272 277229

Getting on

At various points in this book some aspects of career progression within the computing industry have been put before you. Wherever you start there are various possible paths to jobs at higher levels; in many areas people tend to move up in the same firm or over to another one quite quickly. Thus on page 57 one figure shows that in some types of work the annual staff turnover is between a fifth and a quarter. In some cases the value can reach 50 per cent or even higher. The figure below refers mainly to people in permanent posts in data processing, and shows much the same thing in a different way. Based on a mid-1986 survey, it gives the length of time people had spent in their previous posts.

Length of time spent by permanent computer staff in their last job

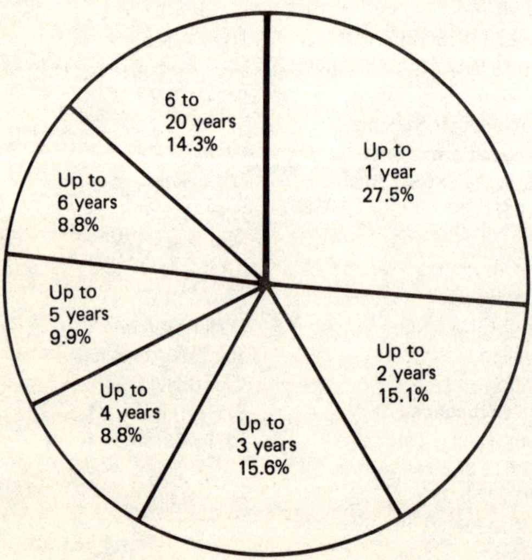

Why do people move so fast? Despite earlier comments about the fairly high rate of increase in pay, money is not the main reason, as the figure below shows. The need to widen experience seems to come first in most such people's minds and this may indicate a certain boredom with their work (though when asked, few said that this is the case).

Main reasons for changing job

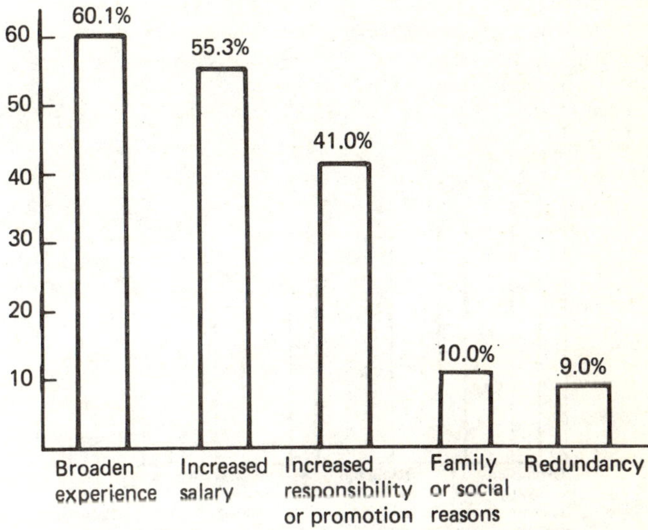

Despite the importance of wider experience, the survey appeared to find that most people did not have clear ideas about where they wanted to go in the future and what they wanted to be doing. Broadly speaking, over a third expected to reach management status, whereas nearly a third reckoned they would turn freelance. All the same, these ideas were not clear-cut and it seems that most people's plans and hopes for the next few years involve no more than a step or two up.

One can see that these attitudes partly follow the rapidly changing nature of the industry: after all, no one can imagine what data-processing work will be like in a quarter of a century. Partly, too, it follows the lack of training offered by many employers, a lack mentioned already more than once. Indeed, the same survey indicated that almost a third of the people involved had received no training at all in the previous two years, and, of those who had, 10 per cent arranged and paid for it themselves. Admittedly, most of that last group were contract staff (freelances and such who would have to do their own thing far more as far as further training is concerned).

Training methods experienced

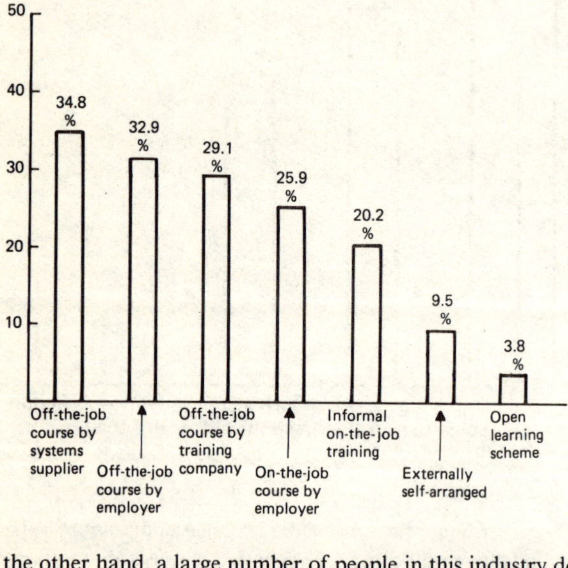

On the other hand, a large number of people in this industry do not seem to think that further training is needed; they believe they will pick up what they require from experience as they go on working. In a sense they may be right, because one of the most interesting findings of the survey is that three-quarters of the respondents did not have the qualifications required for their present job when they applied for it. If that is a general pattern it means that you should not hesitate to go for jobs a level or two up on your current position, even if you do not fit the description closely.

Chapter 10

Further and Higher Education and Training

Qualifications related to information processing that may be obtained range from basic ones in programming to degrees in computer science and allied subjects. Some of the many main such qualifications are described below, and lists of educational establishments from which further details may be obtained follow.

City and Guilds Basic Programming Certificate

This is typical of a number of useful low-level qualifications that potential employers appreciate. In this case certificates are awarded jointly by the National Computing Centre and the City and Guilds of London Institute, who have worked together in making this subject an on-demand examination. This means that recognised centres can hold the examination when they wish, to suit the short courses needed by various organisations. The scheme is intended for trainee and junior programmers seeking employment in computer departments. Although this is not essential for entry, it is good if you have O levels or equivalent qualifications in English and mathematics. You can get a list of colleges which offer courses leading to this examination from the City and Guilds of London Institute, 76 Portland Place, London W1N 4AA (01-580 3050). More and more schools offer them too.

Perhaps the most exciting of the other relevent City and Guilds courses is 444 Inside Information. Developed in conjunction with the BBC this too leads to a certificate that is offered on-demand by a number of centres. (Even more interestingly, it is one that is obtained after success at an assessment administered by computer.) Inside Information covers the whole area of information technology to a fair depth, though it is not highly technical. Contact the City and Guilds Institute (address above) to find out which colleges and schools in your area offer courses leading to this certificate.

Royal Society of Arts Computer Operations/Data Preparation and Handling

The RSA holds examinations in both the above subjects. The course for the Computer Operations Certificate lasts one year part-time or four months full-time. There are no entry requirements but it is assumed that the student is already working with computers and, again, an English qualification helps. RSA stages I and II Data Preparation and Handling may also be followed part-time or full-time. Examinations are held at each stage. Get full details of course content and where the courses are held from the Royal Society of Arts, John Adam Street, London WC2N 6EZ (01-839 1691). You can also find out from them about other useful RSA courses.

London Chamber of Commerce and Industry Certification

The LCCI oversees courses in commerce and business at a number of levels through centres all over the world. These courses lead to certificates and diplomas that are highly regarded though they often require a great deal of work. In each case a number of separate areas must be explored, with computing and related subjects being on offer too. You can get further details from the LCCI at Marlowe House, Station Road, Sidcup, Kent DA15 7BJ (01-302 0261). Also, they will let you know which colleges offer teaching in these areas; there are many of them.

This chapter up to now has only scratched the surface as far as low and intermediate qualifications are concerned. Seek further advice on these and other courses from your library, nearby colleges or from the Manpower Services Commission. If your area has a TAPS point (a computerised database of training opportunities), use it. This section will close with contact details of the Pitman Examinations Institute, a long-lived provider of relevant high-quality courses at this level; write to the Institute at Godalming, Surrey GU7 1UU (04868 5311).

The Business and Technician Education Council National Diplomas and Certificates

In the early 1970s the Business Education Council (BEC) and Technician Education Council (TEC) were set up by the government to provide a unified national (England and Wales) system of non-degree courses. Together they established a series of courses leading to awards in computer studies among other things, and in 1983 were merged to form the Business and Technician Education Council (BTEC). As a result of this merger a new series of awards were defined as follows. These apply to England and Wales studies only. Details of the Scottish equivalent, SCOTVEC, are given on page 124.

BTEC General Certificate and *Diploma in Business Studies* (for young people aged 16–19 years with few academic qualifications).
BTEC National Certificate and *Diploma in Business Studies* (replacing ONC and OND, the certificate is two years part-time while the diploma takes two years full-time or three years part-time).
BTEC Higher National Certificate and Diploma in Business Studies (replacing HNC and HND, the certificate is a two-year part-time course and the diploma lasts two years full-time or three years part-time).

While the above courses contain computing and data processing options, the following are more specifically computer orientated:

BTEC National Certificate and *Diploma in Computer Studies* (certificate one year full-time, two years part-time or 42-week sandwich course and diploma two years full-time, three years part-time).

BTEC Higher National Certificate and *Diploma in Computer Studies* (certificate two years part-time and diploma two years full-time or three years part-time).

It is also possible to study for National Diplomas in Business Studies with a computer option included; many employers consider training of this nature to be as acceptable as pure computer study because you acquire a broader commercial base. You can get details of these examinations, entry requirements and colleges offering appropriate training from the Business and Technicians Education Council at Central House, Upper Woburn Place, London WC1H 0HH (01-388 3288).

The Scottish Vocational Education Council

If you live in Scotland, or intend to study at this level there, you should approach the equivalent organisation. This is SCOTVEC, 38 Queen Street, Glasgow G1 3DY (041-248 7900).

Award of the *Scottish National Certificate* follows work on a modular course, the modules on offer including a total of over 30 in computing, information technology, systems, applications and programming. The courses are provided at all colleges and many schools and also can form part of the work in the Youth Training Scheme and adult training and retraining programmes. Some, indeed, may be studied at home.

SCOTVEC, like BTEC, also offer courses at higher level through colleges of further education and the central institutes. In particular there are the *Higher National Certificate* and the *Higher National Diploma*.

Polytechnic Courses

Polytechnic colleges offer a very wide range of courses at somewhat higher level than the above. These include diplomas and degrees. Their degree courses are fairly new, so the next few paragraphs will concentrate on this degree work.

THE COUNCIL FOR NATIONAL ACADEMIC AWARDS

The CNAA is the largest single degree awarding body in Britain; about one-third of all students who are studying for a degree attend CNAA approved courses. These degrees are fully comparable in standard with those awarded by universities, but the institutions involved are polytechnics and colleges of higher education.

If you plan to work towards a degree in an information technology related area, you should give very serious consideration to the polytechnic system. While being a university undergraduate can be more exciting, and having a university degree gives a certain snob value, most employers now believe that the polytechnic courses are quite a lot more relevant to their actual needs. This picture is bound to change as universities realise they are losing good students to the polytechnics but at the moment university courses on the whole are more theoretical and less practical. This makes them good perhaps for people hoping to become top-class programmers and hardware designers for instance, but not so good for those interested in applications and work with data-processing departments.

While each polytechnic degree course will have been approved by the CNAA, its content will not be standard; write for full details direct to the college(s) in which you are interested. In the following list the phone numbers only of the colleges are given; you can ring for the addresses you need or look them up in the *PCAS Handbook*.

Entry requirements vary as well and you'll need to confirm the particular requirements for each course with the individual colleges. Although most pure computer courses do not require a pass in a mathematical subject at A level, it is needed for courses in mathematics with computing, operational research with computing and statistics with computing. Courses in information systems and systems analysis specify GCSE mathematics, as do most in computing/computer science. The part-time courses are designed for mature students, so colleges will accept a variety of qualifications which show mathematical competence.

Listed below are polytechnics and the courses they offer in computing and allied subjects (summarised on page 131). However, they also have modular courses in which computing or information technology can be a major subject of study for diploma or degree. In addition, there are courses offered by colleges and institutes of higher education; write to SCDP at Edge Hill College, Ormskirk, Lancashire L39 4QP, for a guide book that gives details of these.

KEY TO ABBREVIATIONS

BA	Bachelor of Arts
BEd	Bachelor of Education
BSc	Bachelor of Science
DipHE	Diploma of Higher Education
ft	full-time
pt	part-time

Sandwich courses combine academic study with practical training or supervised work experience in the relevant industry, profession or service. There are two kinds as follows.

T 'Thick' sandwich: a course in which there are typically two years of academic study, followed by a calendar year of supervised work experience, and then a final year of academic study.

tn 'Thin' sandwich: a course with a greater interleaving of academic study and supervised work experience, either on the basis of three six-month periods spent in industry, or with two, the latter usually being considerably longer than six months.

Birmingham Polytechnic 021-356 6911
Computing information systems
BSc/BSc Honours T (4 years)
Industrial information technology
BSc/BSc Honours ft (3 years)

Brighton Polytechnic 0273 693655
Computer studies
BSc/BSc Honours T (4 years)
DipHE ft (2 years)

Microelectronics and information processing
BSc/BSc Honours T (4 years)

Bristol Polytechnic 0272 653221
Systems analysis
BA tn (4 years)
Microelectronics, computing and instrumentation
BSc/BSc Honours T (4 years)

Polytechnic of Central London 01-580 2020
Computer technology
BSc/BSc Honours ft (3 or 4 years)
Control and computer engineering
BEng/BEng Honours ft (3 or 4 years)

City of London Polytechnic 01-283 1030
Computing
DipHE ft (2 years)

Coventry (Lanchester) Polytechnic 0203 24166
Computer science
BSc/BSc Honours tn (4 years)
Computer and control systems
BEng/BEng Honours ft (3 years) or T (4 years)

Glasgow College of Technology 041-332 7090
Information systems
BSc ft (3½ years)

Gloucestershire College of Arts and Technology 0452 35881
Computing
BSc pt (4–6 years)

Hatfield Polytechnic 07072 79000
Computer science
BSc/BSc Honours tn (4 years) or pt

Huddersfield Polytechnic 0484 22288
Computing in business
BA/BA Honours T (4 years)

Kingston Polytechnic 01-549 1141
Computer science
BSc/BSc Honours tn (4 years)
Information systems design
BSc/BSc Honours T (4 years)

Lancashire Polytechnic 0772 22141
Business information technology
BSc Honours T (4 years)
Industrial information technology
BSc/BSc Honours ft (3 years)

Leeds Polytechnic 0532 462903
Operational research and computing
BSc/BSc Honours T (4 years)

Leicester Polytechnic 0533 551551
Computer science
BSc/BSc Honours T (4 years)
Information technology
BSc/BSc Honours T (4 years)

Liverpool Polytechnic 051-207 3581
Computer studies
BSc/BSc Honours T (4 years)

Manchester Polytechnic 061-228 6171
Information technology/Information technology in business
BSc/BSc Honours T (4 years)

Middlesex Polytechnic 01-886 6599
Information technology
in various modular courses

Napier College, Edinburgh 031-443 6061
Computing and data processing
BSc T (4 years)

Newcastle Polytechnic 0632 326002
Computing for industry
BSc/Bsc Honours T (4 years)

North East London Polytechnic 01-590 7722
Computer studies
BA/BA Honours T (4 years)

Polytechnic of North London 01-607 2789
Statistics, mathematics and computing
BSc/BSc Honours T (4 years) or ft (3 years)

North Staffordshire Polytechnic 0785 45531
Computing science/Information systems/Information technology
BSc/BSc Honours T (4 years)
DipHE ft (2 years)

Oxford Polytechnic 0865 64777
Computer studies
within various modular courses

Paisley College of Technology 041-887 1241
Computing science
BSc/BSc Honours tn (4–5 years)

Plymouth Polytechnic 0752 221312
Computing and informatics
BSc/BSc Honours T (4 years)

Portsmouth Polytechnic 0705 827681
Computer science
BSc/BSc Honours T (4 years)
Information technology and society
BSc Honours ft (3 years)

Sheffield City Polytechnic 0742 20911
Computer studies
BSc/BSc Honours T (4 years)

Information technology
BSc/BSc Honours T (4 years)

South Bank Polytechnic, London 01-928 8989
Computing studies
BSc/BSc Honours T (4 years)
Computer and information engineering
BEng/BEng Honours T (4 years) or ft ($3\frac{1}{2}$ years) or pt

Sunderland Polytechnic 0783 76231
Data processing
BA/BA Honours T (4 years)

Teesside Polytechnic 0642 218121
Computer technology
BEng/BEng Honours T (4 years) or ft (3 years)
Computer science/Computer studies
BSc/BSc Honours T (4 years)

Thames Polytechnic, London 01-854 2030
Computer and communications systems
BSc/BSc Honours T (4 years)
Computing science
BSc/BSc Honours T (4 years) or pt

Ulster Polytechnic 0231 65131
Computer science (data processing)
BSc/BSc Honours T (4 years)

Polytechnic of Wales 0443 405133
Computer studies
BSc/BSc Honours T (4 years) or pt
DipHE ft (2 years)
Information technology
BSc/BSc Honours T (4 years)
DipHE ft (2 years)

Wolverhampton Polytechnic 0902 710654
Computer science
DipHE ft (2 years) or pt (3 years)

	Computer Science or Studies	Information Technology or Systems Design	Maths, Statistics & Computing	Systems Analysis or Information	Communication or Information Systems	Computer Aided
Birmingham	□			•		
Brighton	□●	□	●	o		
Bristol	□o	-•-	□	•	o	
Coventry Lanchester	□•		□		-•-	
Hatfield	□●	□	□	o		
Huddersfield	□●	□●		□●		
Kingston	•	-•-		•		
Lancashire	□o	□•	□			□
Leeds	□•	□	□		•	
Leicester	□●	□●	□●	o	o	
Liverpool	□●		•			
London: Central	□●		o			□
London: City of	o	o	●	o		
London: North	●		□●	o	●	
London: South Bank	□●					
London: Thames	□●		□●	o	•	
Manchester	□o	•	□			
Middlesex			o			
Newcastle upon Tyne	□	□				
North East London	□●		●			
N. Staffordshire	□●	•		•		□•
Oxford	□o		•			
Plymouth	□•		o		●	
Portsmouth	□•		□	o		
Sheffield	□•	•	□	•		□
Sunderland	□●	•				
Teesside	□●	□o	□	o		□
Trent	□o					
Wales	□●	•	□●			□
Wolverhampton	□●		●	o		

• *Degree or recognised equivalent course with specialisation (or majoring) in named subject area*

o *Joint/Combined Degree with named subject as one of the main areas of study*

□ *Higher National Diploma course in named subject area*

University Degree Courses

Before you go too far in thinking about university degree course entry, read the comments about the value of their work at the beginning of the previous section on polytechnics. The minimum entry requirements for first degree courses at a university are, usually, a specific number of GCSE pass grades and at least two A levels, one of which, in most cases, should be in mathematics. The combination of subjects comprising each university's course varies considerably and it is beyond the scope of this book to list them in detail. Listed below are the phone numbers of universities which offer first-degree courses that contain at least a third of computer study. You can get further details from the registrar of the university concerned. (Through the same numbers you can also find out about the services available for placing graduates in posts. This is part of the work of the Central Services Unit mentioned in Chapter 7.)

No two university courses are alike, though there will be a basic core of material common to most if not all. All the courses, however, provide a good general background in the subject, and probably you will also have to follow relevant subsidiary subjects as well. Often you have the chance to specialise in an area of particular interest in the last year of the course.

Finally, note that more and more universities offer sandwich courses, ones with a lengthy period of practical work in the industry as described for polytechnic work. Certainly, if you have a particular interest in mind you should study the course details with great care. Then you can choose a department which offers that area among its study options and/or among its research interests. You will need to give prospectuses careful study too if you want an applied rather than theoretical bias to your work, or if you would welcome doing some research as part of the course.

Aberdeen 0224 40241
Aberystwyth 0970 3111
Aston (Birmingham) 021-359 3611
Birmingham 021-472 1301
Bradford 0274 33466
Brighton 0273 606755

Bristol 0272 24161
Brunel 0895 37188
Cambridge 0223 358933
Canterbury 0227 66822
Cardiff 0222 44211
City (London) 01-253 4399
Colchester 0206 862286
Coventry 0203 24011
Dundee 0382 23181
Durham 0385 64466
Edinburgh 031-667 1081
Exeter 0392 77911
Glasgow 041-339 8855
Heriot-Watt (Edinburgh) 031-225 8432
Hull 0482 46311
Institute of Science and Technology (Manchester) 061-236 3311
Keele 0782 621111
Lancaster 0524 65201
Leeds 0532 31751
Liverpool 051-709 6022
London
- Birbeck College 01-580 6622
- Chelsea College 01-351 2488
- Imperial College 01-589 5111
- King's College 01-351 2488/836 5454
- London School of Economics 01-405 7686
- Queen Elizabeth College 01-937 5411
- Queen Mary College 01-980 4811
- Royal Holloway College 07843 4455
- University College 01-387 7050
- Westfield College 01-435 7141

Loughborough 0509 63171
Manchester 061-273 3333
Newcastle 0632 28511
Norwich 0603 56161
Nottingham 0602 506101
Open University 0908 74066
Oxford 0865 56747
Reading 0734 85123

St Andrews 0334 76161
Salford 061-736 5843
Sheffield 0742 78555
Southampton 0703 559122
Stirling 0786 3171
Strathclyde (Glasgow) 041-552 4400
Surrey 0483 71281
Swansea 0792 25678
York 0904 59861

Chapter 11

Further Sources of Help

This is rather a rag-bag of ideas of places where you can find out more about information technology (IT) and work within those industries. It is fitting to start with some electronic sources of relevant information.

TAPs

At the time of writing, the Manpower Services Commission is extending the TAPs scheme. Eventually, these 'training access points' will be common around the country. The intention is to provide, through an interactive computer system, details of all kinds of training opportunities nationally and for each area. TAPs are being set up in such places as public libraries and shopping centres; contact your careers service, library, Citizens' Advice Bureau, Jobcentre or MSC office to find if the scheme exists in your area.

LISA

This is Library and Information Science Abstracts, a dial-in electronic database covering developments in information technology. If you can visit a large public or university library you may be able to see it. LISA is expensive, however.

Prestel

If you have access to Prestel (at school/college, home or library) you will find a great deal of help on careers. Much of this is provided by an MSC department, COIC (the Careers and

Occupational Information Centre). You can start with COIC on Prestel page *270 as well as finding other leads through pages *182 (Prestel Careers Guidance) and *8882 (Prestel Education Careers Information).

Times Network

This is another dial-up database that includes useful careers advice in its services and is common in schools and colleges.

COIC

As well as putting a lot of information on to Prestel, COIC offer many other aids to careers and training. These include computer programs and books and booklets. COIC often take stands at careers exhibitions; you can get in touch with them through your local MSC office or at Moorfoot, Sheffield S1 4PQ (0742 753275). Find out too about their DOORS (data on occupations retrieval system), a splendid careers database on computer.

CRAC

This is the Careers Research and Advice Centre, also a prolific publisher of useful materials (including some excellent video cassettes on careers in IT and on applying for jobs). CRAC are at Bateman Street, Cambridge CB1 1LZ (0233 354551).

Careers Service

Of course, this remains your main source of advice. Not only can the staff offer you direct personal help and put you in touch with others to do the same, but you will find they have a wealth of literature. You can work through COIC's *Signposts* material (on computer and backed by a resource bank of information cards), check through their lists of sources of free literature and possible employers and funders, study the AGCAS guide to opportunities for graduates and so on. Look up Careers Service in your local phone book.

NCC

The National Computer Centre is on Oxford Road, Manchester M1 7ED (061-228 6333). It plays a major role in training and careers advice as far as computing and IT are concerned; many of its publications should be available at your careers office and central library. Through its regional offices the NCC also offers a valuable job-hunter assessment service designed to match you as closely as possible to the needs of potential employers. The NCC also publishes typical job descriptions of personnel in data processing and preparation departments.

BCS

The British Computing Society have a very high membership among professional people in our areas of interest. Particularly, if you are a graduate working full-time with computers, you should consider membership. In exchange you gain access to their many useful publications and have the chance of helping the industry to move the way you want through one of the society's many working groups. Like the NCC, the BCS plays a major part in ensuring the professionalism of employers and staff in the industry. An important new initiative in this direction is to devise job standards (codes of practice) to match the NCC's job descriptions. At the time of writing there are about 80 jobs covered by the scheme and the descriptions are coming to be accepted by training organisations. BCS also look after the NCC Basic Certificate in Systems Analysis, an important qualification obtained by examination; it is much the same as the MSC's own Systems Analysis course. BCS's own professional qualification confers a rank equivalent to a chartered engineer or scientist. Part I involves sitting two compulsory papers and two specialist ones chosen from a list of eight; it is roughly equivalent to a relevant DipHE, ordinary degree or HND. You can register for the examination if you have five GCSE passes or equivalent (including English and mathematics), one A level, and at least a year's relevant experience. Part II can be taken either by written and oral examination or by writing and discussing a dissertation (long essay) about original work. The part II qualification is equivalent to an honours degree. The address of the British Computer Society is 13 Mansfield Street, London W1M 0BP (phone 01-637 0471 to find out about any of the above or their various grades of membership).

IDPM

The Institute of Data Processing Management is another professional association, this time for people working at fairly high level in the industry. Indeed, it was the first body to set up professional qualification by exam in this field (a quarter of a century ago). Parts I and II give qualifications equivalent to ONC, and parts III and IV are about HNC standard. To start up this ladder you need four GCSE passes (including mathematics or science and English) or have two years' relevant experience. The IDPM headquarters is at 18 Henrietta Street, London WC2E 8NU (01-240 3305).

OU

The Open University has been providing degree courses by distance education (home study) for nearly 20 years. An OU degree (ordinary or honours) is equivalent in standard to one from a traditional university or a polytechnic. As with all the courses mentioned here, to be successful requires great determination. Whether you are full-time at home or at work it is not easy to keep up with the course and the assessments and to revise for the exams. To obtain an OU degree you need to collect credits from a number of courses over several years. Each course requires you to do adequately well in a number of assignments during the year and to pass an exam in the autumn (courses start in January); in some cases you will also be assessed during a week's residential practical workshop on campus. All the courses are based on special course books which thump on to your doormat every month or two; there may as well be radio and TV broadcasts (also available on cassette) and you can attend classes and discussion groups at a study centre. Many courses involve the use of a computer, normally a terminal at a study centre, and if that is the case, that is assessed too. It is less well known that the OU offers many courses in special non-degree packages or as stand-alone opportunities for study by 'associate students'. The following courses might interest you particularly:

The digital computer
Computing and computers
Learning about microcomputers
Inside microcomputers
Software engineering
Computer architecture and operating systems
Real-time monitoring
Systems modeling
Real-time control
Project management
Commercial data processing with COBOL
Structured programming with Pascal
Computer-based information systems
Introduction to systems analysis and design
Data analysis for information system design

Other Useful Contacts

Association of Computer Machinery
c/o EOSYS
Clove House
The Broadway
Farnham Common
Buckinghamshire SL2 3PQ
02814 51232

Association of Professional Computer Consultants (APCC)
109 Baker Street
London W1M 2BH
01-267 7144

British Microcomputer Manufacturers Group (BMMG)
Owles Hall
Buntingford
Hertfordshire SG9 9PL
0763 71209

British Robot Association (BRA)
28–30 High Street
Kempston
Bedfordshire MK42 7AJ
0234 853605

CADCAM Association
PO Box 111
Middlesbrough
Cleveland TS1 2LX
0642 244567

Computer and Peripherals Equipment Trade Association (COMPETA)
Owles Hall
Buntingford
Hertfordshire SG9 9PL
0763 71209

Computer Retailers Association
Owles Hall
Buntingford
Hertfordshire SG9 9PL
0763 71209

Computing Services Association (CSA)
Hanover House
73–74 High Holborn
London WC1V 6LE
01-405 2171

Computing Services Industry Training Council (COSIT)
Victoria House
Vernon Place
London WC1B 4DP
01–242 5049

Institute of Administrative Management (IAM)
40 Chatsworth Parade

Petts Wood
Kent BR15 1RW
0689 75555

Institute of Management Consultants (IMC)
Alfred House
23-24 Cromwell Place
London SW7 2LG
01-584 7285

Institute of Management Services (IMS)
1 Cecil Court
London Road
Enfield
Middlesex EN2 6DD
01-363 7452

Institution of Analysts and Programmers
Gibson House
39–41 Fourth Cross Road
Twickenham
Middlesex TW2 5EL
01-898 0195

Institution of Electrical Engineers (IEE)
Savoy Place
London WC2R 0BL

Management Consultancies Association (MCA)
11 West Halkin Street
London SW1X 8JL
01-235 3897

NCR Computer Users Association
c/o De Havilland College
Elstree Way
Borehamwood
Hertfordshire WD6 1JZ
01-953 6024

UNIX/usr/group/UK
8 Chequer Street
St Albans
Hertfordshire AL1 3XZ
0727 38138

Wang (UK) User Group
6–12 Norton Folgate
London E1 6BN
01-247 7661

Going to the Fair

A fairly new sight in the computer world is the computer recruitment fair, of which there seem to be more and more each year (mainly, alas, in London). Companies wanting data-processing staff look after stands and report very high success rates in filling their vacancies from the throng of visitors. Mind you, their personnel staff can sometimes be rather embarrassed to see their own people looking at what their competitors want. Visit a computer fair if you can, as you will learn a great deal about the industry. The chances of finding a (new) job are often high too: a large two-day fair may have a hundred stands with over a thousand jobs on offer. Even the smaller open evenings can attract a dozen or two companies. Computer fairs are advertised in specialist papers like *Computer Weekly*.

DONT

DONT is the Kogan Page *Directory of Opportunities in New Technology* (£7.95), the second edition of which appeared in 1986. Covering computer programming and service, electronic and electrical engineering, telecommunications and information technology, the book is aimed particularly at graduates and people thinking of study for a degree at university or polytechnic. The directory lists possible major employers, postgraduate courses and companies that offer sponsorship to students. When you get to *DONT* in your library (its classification is 602.3) see if there are any other reference books of interest on the same shelf.

Times Courses Review

After the A level results appear colleges find themselves with places to fill. You can work out the reasons. For several weeks around the end of August *The Times* and the *Sunday Times* carry details of vacancies on courses. They may be worth looking at if you're at a loose end; if you're enthusiastic you may be able to get a good place even if you didn't pass any A level examinations.

Books

There are thousands of books on computing and information technology. Do visit your local libraries and bookshops and browse, borrow or buy. Here are details of a few particularly recommended books that give a useful extra background knowledge.

The Software Business by Meyer Soloman (BBC, 1986): 'how to create, publish and sell computer software'; very good and useful reading.
Inside Information by Jacquetta Megarry (BBC, 1985) : an extremely detailed but easy to read opening introduction to IT (there are also two audio tapes).
The Microelectronics Revolution by Tom Forester (Blackwell, 1980): somewhat dated now, alas, but a very important and informative collection of about 60 papers on IT and society.
The Automated Office by Joseph Bate (Collins, 1985): a good introduction.
Supervising the Electronic Office by Caroline Blaazer (Gower, 1984): very expensive but provides a solid though brief overview.
Information Technology at Work by Dick Davies (Heinemann, 1986): an outstanding textbook at GCSE level.
About Information Technology (Hobsons, 1986): a very easy-to-read coverage of the basics of the subject.
Computer World by Jacquetta Megarry (Kingfisher/Piccolo, 1983): just the thing to slip into your pocket as you leave for an interview; a simple and very useful introduction.
Advanced Word Processing and the Electronic Office by Joyce Stananought (McGraw-Hill, 1986): a very good (though not well

written) course on modern technology in the office for people with some experience.

Business Data Systems by H D Clifton (Prentice-Hall, 1983): dreary but thorough.